Ten Traditional Tellers

REVIEW COPY

Ten Traditional Tellers
Margaret Read MacDonald

U.S. Cloth Price: $50
U.S. Paper Price: $20
Publication Date: May 29, 2006

Contact: Michael Roux, (217) 244-4689
mroux@uillinois.edu

Please send TWO copies of your review to:

University of Illinois Press
1325 South Oak Street
Champaign, IL 61820-6903
Fax: (217) 244-8082
www.press.uillinois.edu

Ten Traditional Tellers

Margaret Read MacDonald

UNIVERSITY OF ILLINOIS PRESS

Urbana and Chicago

Library of Congress Cataloging-in-Publication Data
MacDonald, Margaret Read, 1940–
Ten traditional tellers/ Margaret Read MacDonald.
p. cm.
Includes bibliographical references and index.
ISBN-13: 978-0-252-03055-0 (cloth: alk. paper)
ISBN-10: 0-252-03055-9 (cloth: alk. paper)
ISBN-13: 978-0-252-07297-0 (pbk: alk. paper)
ISBN-10: 0-252-07297-9 (pbk: alk. paper)
1. Tales—Cross-cultural studies. 2. Storytelling—
Cross-cultural studies. I. Title.
GR67.M23   2006
398.2—dc22
2005035212

Contents

Preface

About This Project

From 1978 to 1985, I worked rather incessantly at taping and transcribing the storytelling events of my mother's hometown, Scipio, Indiana. I learned much about storytelling style, audience response, and the way a community plays with a tale. I put it all together in *Scipio Storytelling: Talk in a Southern Indiana Community* (University Press of America, 1996). But I was still curious. Slowly I began to record the comments of tellers I met who had grown out of traditional backgrounds. I wanted to hear more of the traditional teller's voice. I wanted not only stories but commentary about the storytelling. Why do these folks tell? For whom? What started them on the teller's path?

During these many interviews I encouraged comments from the tellers about their approach to the storytelling art. In chapter 12 I ponder the reasons these tellers have for telling stories, and I ask the question, How traditional are these tellers?

In 1986 and 1987 the Seattle Storytellers' Guild and the Washington State Folklife Council organized a Traditional Tellers Retreat, an event at which we connected teachers and librarians with traditional storytellers. Liberian teller Won-Ldy Paye, Chehalis teller Curtis DuPuis, Tibetan Rinjing Dorje, and Eskimo elder Lela Oman were among our participants, as was the godmother of Seattle's storytelling community, Lushootseed elder Vi Hilbert. Tapes were made of each session. I then followed up with lengthy interviews with Won-Ldy, Lela, Rinjing, and Vi and with a tape of Curtis's discussion of his tradition at the National Association for the Preservation and Perpetuation of Storytelling 1993 conference in Seattle.

Shortly after I began work on this project, the Ghanian museologist, Peter Pipim stopped through Seattle to lecture at the Seattle Art Museum. His lecture on Akan storytelling fascinated me, and Peter agreed to an interview.

As the years passed, I was fortunate to spend time with several exceptional individuals. At the 1993 Glistening Waters Storytelling Festival in Masterton, New Zealand, I met Léonard Sam. Léonard told, in French, Kanak tales from his native New Caledonia. On tape he talked about Kanak telling traditions and even told one story in Kanak for my pleasure.

Returning from another trip to New Zealand in 1995, I was invited to visit Makia Malo and his wife Ann in their cottage at Kalaupapa settlement on the island of Molokai. This gave us a lovely retreat to talk story. Makia had been a patient at the Hansen's disease settlement at Kalaupapa since his youth, and though he now lives in Honolulu, he still maintains a cottage at Kalaupapa. Later Makia stayed in my home in Seattle on occasions when he came to perform here, and we had more times to talk.

While working as a Fulbright Scholar in Thailand in 1996 and 1997, I was fortunate to be taken by my host to hear stories by Phra Inta Kaweewong at Wat Sa-ahdsomboon in Roi Et Province. This monk was invited annually to our storytelling conferences and our Tellabrations in Mahasarakham, so I got to hear him speak several times and got to know him in several settings.

During a fall 1998 storytelling tour to Brazil, I traveled with the remarkable teller from Belo Horizonte, Roberto Carlos Ramos. The next summer, we were lucky to host Roberto Carlos, Livia de Almeida, and Anna Portella for a week of telling in Seattle. There was time for interviews, with help from the remarkable translation skills of Livia de Almeida.

In preparing this book for publication, I was adamant that the *interviews* receive prime coverage. The tales are fascinating, yes. But we have thousands of folktale collections in our libraries and yet hardly a word from the tellers themselves. I transcribed the tales using an ethnopoetic format so that the line breaks where the teller pauses. In setting the interviews in print, I also used that technique at times to draw attention to paced speech. Here, in the tellers' own words, are their comments on storytelling. If the accompanying tales seem a bit rough, it is because they are transcribed from live tellings. These have not been polished over until, as Lela says, "all the truth and beauty are gone from them." This is the way these folks told it—on one day, when my tape recorder was running.

About the Tellers

The tellers presented in this book all take their telling very seriously. The act of storytelling is an important part of their lives, an integral component of their personas. Taking on the role of storyteller is no small thing. There are stories to learn, enough to make a versatile repertoire. There is the sometimes daunting role of finding and commanding the attention of audiences. There is the effort to keep one's repertoire alive over a lifetime.

Robert J. Adams has presented some useful criteria for a master teller in his doctoral dissertation, "The Social Identity of a Japanese Storyteller" (Folklore Institute, Indiana University, 1972). Adams studied the rural storyteller Mrs. Tsune Watanabe. From his analysis of her life, he suggests factors that cause a person to develop the social identity of a storyteller.

First of all, the potential teller needs to have exposure to other tellers. Usually this young teller-to-be actively seeks out storytelling events, often begging elders to tell stories. The teller-to-be begins to identify with the tellers and eventually decides to shift from the role of listener to that of teller.

For the individual who decides to adopt the role of storyteller, the tales function in specific ways. The teller accepts the stories as valid embodiments of cultural values and beliefs and finds in them a reflection of the teller's own attitudes. The teller then appropriates the stories as a means of personal expression.

Certain abilities are necessary to the master teller. Adams notes the ability to master storytelling techniques, the ability to remember, the ability to shape tales, and the ability to conceptualize and fulfill the demands of the listeners. He mentions also the need of the master teller to gain control of a large enough repertoire to satisfy varying audiences and events.

Adams notes two other very important factors in the creation of a master teller. The teller must have the opportunity to practice storytelling in reinforcing situations. And the community must accept the teller's new social identity as storyteller.

It may be interesting to consider these factors in the creation of a master teller as we read the words of the ten tellers interviewed here.

All of our tellers share tales because they love the act of telling. They clearly enjoy sharing their stories with audiences. All seem to feel a need to pass on their traditions to others. But the basic motivations that cause them to tell again and again reveal nuances as each teller discusses his or her telling. Each of these tellers has a personal and deeply felt reason for telling.

I hope this book will reveal some of the many reasons humans have for sharing story. I hope it will show also that the storytelling experience is unique to each individual. The fine teller is respected because this person reaches down and brings up story from within his or her own *inimitable* persona.

Our tellers are eager to share their tales with audiences. And just as they sought out tellers to listen to in their formative years, they now seek out audiences to whom they can pass on the tales. These folks seem on a *mission* to share stories.

I want these tellers to share with you in their own words. I questioned them about the paths that led them to storytelling and their reasons for telling. But mostly I just let them talk. I later transcribed the interviews and from the transcripts selected their most passionate and revealing moments.

Each chapter contains a brief background about the teller's country or culture, provided for those who approach the teller without previous knowledge of the teller's home region. In the chapter body I offer a brief introduction to the teller, discuss the interview setting, and then let the teller speak. A bibliography of the teller's works is provided at the chapter's end, along with a short list of sources about the teller and the teller's culture, where pertinent titles are available.

Briefly now, let me introduce our ten tellers.

Vi Hilbert is a member of the Upper Skagit tribe of northwestern Washington state. She grew up along the Skagit River in a Lushootseed-speaking environment. Late in life, married and living in Seattle, she was enlisted by University of Washington professors to help transcribe Lushootseed texts. Her life became devoted to this work, and today, in her eighties and though nearly blind, she continues the work. She says, "The creator took my sight so that I could concentrate more on what was important to do." Her storytelling, which grew from her need to share her culture, has taken her throughout North America and abroad to conferences and storytelling festivals.

Rinjing Dorje spent his youth in Tibet and Nepal. Early in life he was pledged to the monkhood, but it proved unsuitable for his temperament. His tales draw more from his days herding sheep than from his life in the monastery. He wants listeners to know that Tibetan culture is broader than just the religious life about which we hear so much. His bawdy tales of Uncle Tompa both shock and delight adult audiences.

Roberto Carlos Ramos was a street child in Belo Horizonte, Brazil. After running away from orphanages more than thirty-two times, he finally was taken in by a French-speaking social worker when he was a teen. She saw to it that he completed his education, but the personal stories that he shares reveal a truly tortuous path to manhood. He now teaches at an orphanage where he was once incarcerated and uses story as a way to reach these troubled youth.

Phra Inta Kaweewong serves as monk in a small rural wat (temple) in northeastern Thailand. He uses story in his sermons to suggest Buddhist moral behavior to his parishioners. He has also devoted much effort to translating tales from old palm leaf manuscripts, which are preserved in many wats. He can read their archaic text and translates them into modern dialects.

Makia Malo spent much of his life at Kalaupapa, the Hansen's disease colony on Molokai Island in Hawaii. After a happy childhood on Hawaiian Homestead lands at Papakoleo, he was sent at age twelve to Kalaupapa. By the time he was released at age thirty-seven, he was blind and physically marked by the disease. He braved the stares he knew were given him by society and went on to earn his bachelor's degree in Hawaiian studies and to begin sharing stories in schools and later at conferences and festivals.

Won-Ldy Paye carries on the storytelling traditions of his griot grandmother, coupled with the drumming tradition of his father. They are of the Dan people. Exiled to the U.S. because of civil wars in his homeland of Liberia, Won-Ldy now makes his way by teaching drumming, touring with his drum ensembles, and telling stories at schools and libraries.

Léonard Sam is a teller from the South Pacific island of New Caledonia. He is of the Kanak people, original inhabitants of these islands, who now make up about 42.5 percent of its population. Leonard teaches at the University of New Caledonia, but he makes time to share in museums and schools stories that he learned from his grandparents.

Lela Oman grew up near Nome, Alaska, hearing stories from friends and relations. As a young mother, she began writing down some of the stories she recalled. Now an elder, she continues to recover as much of the tale-lore as she can from her people. She travels to conferences to speak of her culture and shares some tales within the context of her talk, but mainly she devotes herself to the task of getting these tales down in print.

Peter Pipim grew up in Kumasi, Ghana, heart of the Asante (Ashanti) culture. He is recently retired from a career as educational consultant at the Museum of African Heritage, a division of the Smithsonian Institution in Washington, D.C. Peter has been able to share many stories through his work and also oversee the other storytellers for the museum.

Curtis DuPuis grew up on the Chehalis Reservation in southwestern Washington state. He takes seriously the task of passing his cultural heritage on to his family and spends much time sharing his culture with the extended family of Hazel Pete, his mother. It is not only story that he passes on. Material culture, beliefs, everything passed down from his mother is taught to his family. Curtis tells no stories from other families within his tribe, though he knows many of these stories. He would need permission from the other families to share their stories. But equally important, he fears that learning and telling the tales of other families would contaminate his own family lore. Each family might have different versions of tales. Curtis wants to keep the Hazel Pete tradition intact as it was passed to him. Though he is busy in his work as a contract manager for the State of Washington, Curtis takes time to share his family tales with non-Indians in schools, libraries, and conferences in the area.

These are our tellers. I will let them tell you more about themselves. In chapter 11 I will discuss again the teller's rationales for telling stories. And in chapter 12 I will tackle the question, Why do I consider these ten individuals to be "traditional" tellers?

Acknowledgments

My thanks to the ten tellers whose words are featured in this book. They joyfully gave of their time for interviews and willingly answered the many queries I sent their way since then. My thanks also to Donald Braid and Jo Radner for insightful suggestions that added much to the final form of this book. Thanks to my daughter, Jennifer Whitman, for help in translating Léonard Sam's very fuzzy French tape. And thanks to my editor, Liz Dulany, for seeing a book in this material and shepherding it to press.

Ten Traditional Tellers

Vi Hilbert. Photo courtesy of Paul Eubanks.

1

Vi (taqʷšəblu) Hilbert
Tradition as Responsibility

Important people kept the information alive.
And they knew it was their responsibility.
Just as I know.
  Vi (taqʷšəblu) Hilbert

UPPER SKAGIT TRIBE BACKGROUND

The Upper Skagit Reservation is located in the Cascade Mountain foothills near Sedro Wooley in Skagit County, Washington. The eighty-four-acre reservation is supplemented by another fifteen-acre parcel of commercially zoned land alongside Interstate 5 near Alger.

The Upper Skagit originally had ten villages on the Upper Skagit and Sauk Rivers. The tribe did not receive formal recognition from the U.S. government until the early 1970s. The reservation was established in 1984. Previous to that time, Upper Skagit persons who wished to live on a reservation resided mainly at the Swinhomish Reservation near La Conner, Washington.

The Upper Skagit website has this to say about their history: "Headmen of the Upper Skagit Tribe were among the signatories to the Point Elliott Treaty of 1855. The government said the Upper Skagit were not one group, there were villages that made up the Upper Skagit. Surveyors from the Northern Pacific Railroad crossed Upper Skagit land in 1870. Then came the white settlers. The Upper Skagit people were angered when the white settlers crossed on their lands that held their dead. The Upper Skagit people suffered from diseases from white contact."[1]

The Upper Skagit Reservation population in 2000 was 180 Native Americans. There were 504 enrolled members of the tribe; many live off the reservation.[2]

Meet Vi Hilbert

Vi Hilbert was raised "up-and-down the Skagit River," as she puts it. Her Lushootseed father was a logger and moved wherever there was work. He and Vi's part-French mother doted on Vi, the only survivor of their eight children. Wherever they moved, Vi felt surrounded by the warmth of a happy home. Visiting with relatives, attending church services, working alongside her elders in the berry fields, Vi was surrounded also by the wondrous Lushootseed language. Years later, when Vi was in her sixties, her own two children grown and her career as a secretary for Children's Hospital ended, Professor Thom Hess of the University of Washington would ask her to help transcribe and translate the hours of Lushootseed tape discovered in the Burke Museum archives. Though Vi had heard stories only from her own parents, many of her elders had shared their repertoire on tape during the active collecting efforts of the 1940s and 1950s. Now for the first time Vi heard these tapes. Her life took on a new direction. The storytellers' voices impelled her to rescue their stories from obscurity. Since then Vi has worked incessantly at the transcription and translation of these tapes. She began to teach courses in the Lushootseed language at the University of Washington. And to engage her students more effectively, Vi began to "internalize," as she puts it, some of the stories from the tapes. Gradually word got out that Vi could "tell stories." At first she tried to decline invitations to storytell, sending instead one of her devoted students, Rebecca Chamberlain. Rebecca's work was well received, and she continues to carry on Vi's traditions, but Vi soon discovered that she could not avoid her "responsibility" to carry her culture in person. She has traveled to Hawaii, to England, and to the National Storytelling Festival in Tennessee. Her book *Haboo: Native American Stories from Puget Sound* (University of Washington, 1985) has made the Lushootseed tales of her elders available to a wide audience. *x̌əčusədəʔ ʔə gʷəqʷulč̓əʔ: Aunt Susie Sampson Peter; The Wisdom of a Skagit Elder* (Lushootseed Press, 1995) brought words from the tapes of her aunt Susie Sampson Peter to life, revealing the lost world of Susie's childhood in the 1860s and her friendship with other elders in the 1950s. For years Vi has worked tirelessly transcribing tapes and preparing a Lushootseed lexicon. Today, at eighty-three, though her eyesight is failing, she refuses to cease in this important work.

Vi Hilbert received a National Heritage Fellowship from the National Endowment for the Arts in 1994. In 1989 she was given the Washington State Governor's Heritage Award. In 1994 Seattle University conferred on her an Honorary Doctor of Humanities. These are just a few of the many recognitions given to this extraordinarily hard-working teller.

Talking with Vi

I visited with Vi at her home in South Seattle in September of 1991.[3] We sat at the dining room table looking out over her sunny backyard. A metallic fish mobile swayed in the breeze, and a wind chime tinkled throughout the session. Now and then a jet taking off passed low in the valley beyond Vi's window. A faint apple-buttery tang of recent canning activity hung in the air, and a stack of just-canned fruit from one of Vi's backyard trees occupied the kitchen table. Vi was quiet, erect, soft spoken, and meticulous in her choice of words.

Childhood Tales, Including X-rated

I asked if Vi had heard stories as a child.

When my parents told me stories, it was because I coaxed and badgered and cajoled. And then my dad would do this. And one story after another he would tell me. With X-rated included. And my mother would gasp and say [*under her breath*], "You're *not* going to tell her *that* story!" [*quietly*] "Yes." She could hear this. So he told any kind of story to me. And I delighted in having the privilege of hearing what I realized were X-rated stories. I didn't know how naughty they were. But I knew that because my mother gasped, that these were no-no stories for little girls to hear.

What kind of stories were these?

It would be Mink stories mainly. Because he was proud of his tools. He was proud of his attributes. He had the biggest tool. And he *used* it. [*laughing*] Very sexily. Have you been reading of Geraldo's tell-all exposé about himself? He's sort of a *Mink*. Very sexy. Sexiness and just natural functions of the human body are part of the things that are X-rated.

I had heard Vi say that stories were told only in the home.

It was never done in public. Not in my world. I think it was always an interfamily affair. And as I say, it's not that these stories were aimed at children primarily. They were told to adults also as a part of information exchange.

Because this was a world that had no books or radio or television, why it also had theater. And there had always been people who indulge and enjoy being theatrical. It's just a part of every human race, I think. That people love to play act. Ones who are extroverts and are not afraid of being laughed at, and enjoy making people laugh. My mother loved to make people laugh.

I wondered if Vi's mother ever told stories to other children too.
No, no. I'm the only one that knew the stories.

Telling Styles

Vi recalls her mother telling a story about a boy shooting a chain of arrows.
But I must have been very young when I heard it. And that's all that I remember, but how animated my mother was. Because she was a storyteller like Aunt Susie. She was very vivacious and was a *ham*. Loved to have an audience. And my Dad was very quiet and withdrawn. Never talked too much. Unless he was sort of forced to. Hardly ever raised his voice to be heard.

Did Vi derive her own style more from her mother or father?
I think that probably I try to do what each of them would like to have me do. And I don't think that I'm any one of them. But I think that I'm just trying to incorporate everything that was important in their way of doing things. And I have so much respect and appreciation for the styles because they all differed. My mother being very flamboyant and colorful and imaginative. My Aunt Susie being that kind of storyteller also. Very uninhibited like Johnny [Moses]. And then . . . entertaining an audience and making people laugh. Whereas my Dad was *fact-u-al.* Everything had to be properly, correctly told. And in a very soft, undramatic way. And you had to listen very quietly, because it took him a *long* time. He studied every word before he spoke it. And so he was very wonderful to listen to. But you had to have lots of patience to listen.

William Shelton, who was a Tulalip, came to the Tulalip boarding school. And he told stories to us. That was the very first time I ever heard anybody telling in public. And he was a man who told stories in the Marysville district and the Everett area. So I was quite impressed with his storytelling. However, he did things differently from my parents. He moralized. He told you what you needed to learn from the story. This story was told so you would know how not to be or how to be. This is what this story is telling you. And even then my mind rebelled. [*under her breath*] My parents don't do that.

Aunt Susie didn't do that either. She didn't moralize. There was one story-teller, Martha Lamont, who moralized. And my cousin Patousse, who is dead now too, used to moralize. But he would say, there is a teaching . . . , that is, a follow-up, on every story. Because lots of people won't understand . . . why the story's being told. There is a teaching that follows the story. So he thought that he should do that.

But I personally feel that it's an insult to the intelligence of each human being. Because that's the way I was brought up. And you never insult the intelligence of somebody else. You never intimate that you are smarter than they are. It's just not part of the teachings of my family. Nor of the culture, really. So I was always surprised when somebody would say, "Here's what you are supposed to get from this."

William Shelton's rational for this was, "When you are talking to white people, they don't understand. So when I am talking to white people, I have to explain to them." But I think white people can understand, just as well as anybody. Give people a chance to think for themselves. That's part of the problem in this world.

My students in class say, "You don't tell us what the meaning of the story is, but you guide us to understand what the story is about. And the impor-tance of . . . the reason the story was told. So you have a way of telling us." Well maybe I do. I say look for the symbolism. And search for the metaphors that are imbedded. And search for the humor that's there. Because some people don't always see what's humorous in the culture. The fact that sarcasm can be a form of humor. And when it's applied skillfully, why it's the very best kind of humor.

It is hard to capture sarcasm on paper because so much comes from vocal inflection. The doubt in your voice . . . about this being true. "He's smart." (Is he?) Your voice says . . . "Is he?" I have struggled with that ever since I've been transcribing. Because you cannot describe a feeling appropriately. Or the spirituality that is embedded in so much of the teachings. It's one-on-one transference that cannot transfer to paper. My husband says, "People have to hear you. In person." Because it's the vibration of the person that people pick up on.

It was told to me in Tennessee by a very observant and dear professor who sat and watched me through several performances, and then we had coffee together afterwards. He said, "You know, there is something very revealing about you." He said, "People come to you and give you immediate feedback about how they have felt about what they have heard from you. But there is an additional element. They all have to touch you." A lot of that follows the storytelling. There is a feeling of needing to be in contact. And I am honored. One of those precious gifts that are a bonus.

Aunt Susie Sampson

Vi's transcriptions of the tapes of her Aunt Susie's stories have had a profound effect on her. Though she never heard Aunt Susie tell stories when she was living, this beloved relative lives again for Vi through the tapes found in the collection of the Burke Museum. Here is one little story Vi tells about her Aunt Susie.

Aunt Susie became very old.

She went to live with her son in Tacoma.

She lived in the little bedroom right off the kitchen.

And her daughter-in-law told the story . . . of listening to Aunt Susie.

Aunt Susie would sit in her bedroom.

And all by herself, review the stories that were important to her to remember.

And one day she started to tell a story and she got into it a little ways and . . . "oh no . . . no I told *that* one yesterday."

And so she went back and told one that she had not told to herself recently.

This is indeed the way our people have kept things alive in their minds. You can't let information stay dormant and never revolve it or reuse it and have it stay alive. That's why it's important to tell the stories over and over again and important to pass on the teaching that it has been my privilege to hear. It was so important to her to remember and have people remember.

And this is how our history was kept alive.

Without books.

Important people kept the information alive.

And they knew it was their responsibility.

Just as *I* know.

Aunt Susie felt so sad that most of her grandchildren didn't understand her.

Because they didn't know the language. And she didn't understand English.

If she had to use English it was so frustrating because her vocabulary was limited.

And when her grandchildren would speak, she wouldn't understand them.

And it was just a terrible frustration to her. And she would rail . . . out loud . . . in the language. "What are they going to know to tell *their* grandchildren when they get old?

Because they don't understand what I am telling them . . . what I have to pass on to them. What are they going to tell *their* grandchildren?"

It Takes Time to Listen

Are any of Vi's elders still living?

They are all gone.

It's very sad to make that statement. But everybody that took good care of information of the ancestors at this point . . . are in the other world.

We have a lot of people who are around my age, who carry bits and pieces of the history of our people.

And the right buttons haven't been pushed to get that information.

It takes *Indian time,* like you're taking today.

To sit here and talk to me.

It takes this kind of time, to push all the right buttons to get important information.

And unfortunately I haven't had that kind of time lately.

To go and just sit. And spend hours just visiting with people.

Because people always are going to be able to tell you of something very important,

if you take the time to listen long enough.

It takes patience . . . to listen long enough.

A Responsibility

I never thought that I was blessed with the kind of historical mind that my parents or Aunt Susie had. But again, I have to say I do the best that I can. And that's all the culture expects of me. I don't have their kinds of minds because I wasn't born when they were . . . had the kind of training they did have. But I know what my responsibility is. And I can do the best I can.

I have so much that I need to do yet. It's, all of it, very interesting and very important to *me*. I don't know how interesting it is or how important it is to any of the rest of my people. But when I feel this way I never feel discouraged about it. Because in the back of my mind I know that there is going to be *one* person . . . out of fifty . . . who will have a very burning desire to contact . . . something important of the culture. And they are going to be interested enough to wade through everything that I have put in writing for them to read. And they will search further to listen to things that are on oral tapes . . . in English. And so there will be somebody who's going to be there to pick up all of the gems and jewels that the ancestors left. There's always somebody. Who has that kind of burning interest to contact the important things of the culture. Maybe it won't be one of my own people. Maybe it will be one of my students—who has respected what they have learned from me through the culture. And there are many of those students out there. So I know that nothing *I* will do will ever go to waste. But it's my responsibility to get more of it out there.

And I keep saying, I need to internalize more of these beautiful stories so that I can have a larger variety of teachings to bring forth. Then I think that . . . all of the stories that I have in the computer now (brain) are stories that . . . many people can hear at each telling. People who have never heard before . . . people who are hearing for the second or third time. And the stories become more theirs each time they hear it. *And* they get a better understanding each time they hear it. I know I appreciate hearing a story many many times. Because you never get the same words, under different situations. So I have quit worrying about that. Worrying about getting a bigger and bigger repertoire. There are so many stories that would be beautiful to tell.

I don't really feel like I am qualified. I know the people that are qualified. They're on these tapes. These are the storytellers. And I'm sort of putting myself in a position that I don't feel I qualify for. I don't really think that I can honestly say that I am this kind of a storyteller. And yet I realize that, in order to keep the culture and the stories alive, I have to push that thought aside and do the best I can with my own tools. So that's what I have finally come to realize. That I can never be the storytellers they were. But I can represent them the very best way I can.

Vi Onstage, with the Elders behind Her

And I found this in Tennessee [at the National Storytelling Festival in Jonesborough]. When I made that discovery it has made it much easier for me to do what I do. For that was my *first* public storytelling. And here I was in a great big tent . . . thousands of people . . . and Laura Simms had such confidence . . . in my ability to do this. People believing in me has been the incentive which pushed me out front. Time and time again.

And so
As I stood there
Wondering how in the world I was going to represent my culture in the best way
Each of those storytellers who had originally told their stories
Came to my rescue
And they came forward and told their stories.
And I didn't have to worry about it.

That's what happened.

So that's what happens each time.
So I don't have to *be* there.

You can, my kids would say, "psyche yourself out" if you want to.
If you have the capacity to do that.
And just become a vehicle . . .
That the story's coming through.

So when I can do it that way
I'd say I don't have to pretend to be something that I am not.
I can just represent those people who need their stories to be remembered.
The gift they gave to us.
That's my responsibility.

On Spirituality

Aunt Susie and my dad came from the same family. The same kind of teaching. And they were both from a very spiritually strong family. So was my mother's side of the family. So I inherit the spirituality from my ancestors, even though I was not allowed to become a member of *anything* when I was younger. Because my dad said, "No. You want to join things for the *wrong* reasons, my daughter. When you have time to give your entire life to what you are going to practice. Then you can do it. But you can't join things just because you're curious. That's the wrong reason. And I've never had the time to commit my entire being to any of the religions that are a part of my culture. I have this other work that takes precedence over everything else. I can't do that just halfway. My grandson has said, "Grandma, are you ever going to become a member of one of the churches?" I said, "Not until my work is done. If it's *ever* done." Other people are taking very *good* care of the spirituality of our people. They're doing it honorably. And that doesn't have to be my job. Thank goodness.

Sharing the Tales

Vi encourages others to adopt the stories she translates and pass them on. Though she especially hopes for her own people to carry these tales, she is glad to see others share the stories too.

I appreciate the Makah's philosophy.
Other people say "Turn OFF your tape recorders.
Turn OFF your cameras."
The Makah say, "Turn ON your tape recorders.
Turn ON your cameras.
We are going to tell our stories.
We are going to sing our songs.
Tell our stories. *Sing* our songs.
But know that you will never tell our stories . . . you will never sing our songs . . .
as well as we Makah."

Vi's Tales

Vi told this first story at an educator's conference at the University of Hawaii, Hilo, in 1991. The text below is transcribed from her videotaped lecture, which included several stories. Vi told the story bilingually, delivering each line first in Lushootseed and then in English. Her skillful delivery worked smoothly, as the audience experienced the character's emotions through the Lushootseed text and then heard Vi's English rendition of the action. Only the English text is given below. Thanks to Vi for sharing this lovely videotape, which reveals Vi in performance, inspired by a room full of supportive Hilo listeners.

Vi prefaced her story with this commentary: This story I used in the classroom. For my students you can tell them four times. Even though four is the magic number. Nevertheless, it goes in here and out here. You need to hear this story to know that I am an old-fashioned teacher. When I say, "This is what I want of you," *this* is what I mean. So Great-Grandmother applies the whip with the story. And this was one of the whips.

MUD HEN BUILDS A NEST

A looong time ago . . .
Because that's when our stories take place . . .
A loooong time ago . . .

The Creator had homes for everybody on this earth.
Everybody.
He thought.

And one day he looked down below at the earth that he had created. It seems that the birds do not have homes.

So again the Creator returned to earth.

His face was shining *so* brightly as he walked. Nobody could see him. Nobody *has* seen him ever.

He called *all* of the birds together.

"Come on eagle . . . come on ducks . . . come on crane . . . come on hummingbirds . . . come on *all* of you. Come on!"

I am going to teach each one of you how to build your home.

All of the birds came.
And everyone listened very very intently as the Creator gave them instructions.
All but one.
Mud Swallow.
Mud Swallow just kept yakking to her friends.
Her friends said, "Mud Swallow you better listen. You'd better listen. The Creator is giving us instructions."

"Oooohhh. *Anybody* knows how to build a house.
I don't have to listen."

The Creator finished his instructions.
And he went home.

Now all of the birds busily began to follow his instructions as they built their homes.
All but one.

Mud Swallow got all dolled up in her finery.

She put on her beautiful necklace.
She put a hairband around her head.
Had a feather there in her hair.

She went from house to house.
Visiting with her friends as they built their homes.
She was interrupting their work.

"You'd better get busy and build your house, Mud Swallow."

No, she didn't listen.
She just kept on messing around.

Now they heard,
The Creator is returning.
He wants to see how each of you have built your homes.

Now Mud Swallow got very very concerned.
"What did he say to *me*?
What did he tell me?
How did he tell *me* to build *my* house?"

"Get Away, Mud Swallow.
You didn't listen.
We are not going to tell you what the Creator said to you.
We are busy.
Go away."

So Mud Swallow frantically ran everyplace trying to get somebody to help . . .
to tell her what it was that the Creator had said to her.
Nobody would help her.
They just ignored her.

As she ran her necklace broke and the beads fell all over the ground.
Her feather broke and dangled over one eye.
And she ran helplessly trying to get some help.

"How should she build her house?
What had the Creator said to her?"

As she felt for her beads on the ground,
she felt some soft mud.

"Oooohhh . . . Maybe I could use this mud."

So she took handfuls of mud and she pressed it very tightly between her hands.

And she put this mud up into the tree.

It was a hot day.

In a few moments, her house fell down.

Four times.

"Maybe I didn't press the sand tightly enough with this mud," she said.

So she picked up handfuls of the mud again.

And she pressed it tightly as she could . . . *hard* as she could.

And again she put it up into the tree.

She put it there.

And the sun was shining.

In a few minutes her house dried and crumbled to the ground.

Four times.

So the third time, she picked up handfuls of mud and she could feel some little sticks there on the ground.

She went ahead and pressed the mud as tightly as she could.

Put it up in the tree.

The sun dried the mud and her house fell.

And she thought, "Maybe if I use those little sticks with my mud, my house will be stronger."

So she did this.

She took the sticks and rolled them with the mud.

Now she put this house up in the tree and it stayed there.

Because she had figured out if she put sticks with her mud it would be stronger.

Now the Creator returned.

And he looked at all the homes that had been built by the birds carrying out his instructions.

And he praised every one of them.
He praised them because they had done such a good job.

As he came to Mud Swallow she was standing there looking very very worried.
"What is the Creator going to say to me?"
The Creator looked at her and he looked at her mud house . . .
And he said, "Mud Swallow,
Because you didn't listen,
Forever and ever you are going to live in this mud house."

And to this day Mud Swallow still lives in a mud house.

That is the end of the story.

You may say, "Habu."

LADY LOUSE

Vi has adopted the little story of Lady Louse as her signature tale. She refuses to tell anyone what "Lady Louse" is all about. Instead, she asks each person to create their own lady louse story. This approach delights Vi so much that she arranged to have a book published with many versions of lady louse written by her students. Here is her "Lady Louse." The story was originally told by Elizabeth Krise to Thomas Hess on the Tulalip Reservation in 1962. The Lushootseed text is given in Vi's book, Lady Louse Lived There *(Lushootseed Press, 1996).*

Lady Louse lived there in that great big house!
All alone.
She had no friends or relatives.
Then she took it.
And she swept it.
That great big house.
There was lots of dirt!
When she got to the very middle of the house,
she got lost!
That was the end of Lady Louse!
That is the end.

Notes

1. The North Region EMS and Trauma Care Council, "Upper Skagit Tribe," http://www.northregionems.com/native/Upper%20Skagit%20Tribe.htm.
2. Northwest Area Foundation Indicator Website, www.indicators.nwaf.org.
3. Interview by Margaret Read MacDonald with Vi Hilbert at her home in Des Moines, Washington, September 13, 1991. Two tapes, in possession of interviewer.

Bibliography

Note that several books are produced by Vi's own press, Lushootseed Press, founded to continue her work.

Bates, Dawn, Thom Hess, and Vi Hilbert. *Lushootseed Dictionary.* Edited by Dawn Bates. Seattle: University of Washington Press, 1994.

Bierwert, Chrisca. *Lushootseed Texts: An Introduction to Puget Salish Narrative Aesthetics.* Lincoln: University of Nebraska Press, 1996.

Hess, Thom, and Vi Hilbert. *Lushootseed: The Language of the Skagit, Nisqually, and Other Tribes of Puget Sound.* Seattle, Wash.: Daybreak Star Press, 1980.

Hilbert, Vi. *Coyote and Rock and Other Lushootseed Stories.* Cassette recording, told by Vi Hilbert. New York: Parabola/HarperCollins, 1992.

———. *Haboo: Native American Stories from Puget Sound.* Translated and edited by Vi (taqʷšəblu) Hilbert. Illustrated by Ron Hilbert/Coy. Seattle: University of Washington Press, 1985.

———. *Huboo: Lushootseed Literature in English.* Vi (taqʷšəblu) Hilbert. © 1980 Vi (taqʷšəblu) Hilbert.

———. *Lady Louse Lived There.* Compiled by Vi (taqʷšəblu) Hilbert, edited by Janet Yoder. Bow, Wash.: Lushootseed Press, 1996.

———. "Lushootseed Language and Story Revival." In *Traditional Storytelling Today,* ed. Margaret Read MacDonald, 383–84. Chicago: Fitzroy-Dearborn, 1999.

———. "On Transcribing the Metcalf Tapes." In *Proceedings of the IXth International Conference on Salishan Languages. August 12–14, 1974,* 49–52. Vancouver: University of British Columbia Press, 1974.

Hilbert, Vi, and Crisca Bierwert. *Ways of the Lushootseed People: Ceremonies & Traditions of Northern Puget Sound Indians.* Seattle, Wash.: United Indians of All Tribes Foundation, 1980.

Hilbert, Vi, and Thom Hess. "Lushootseed." *International Journal of American Linguistics—Native American Texts Series* 2(3) (1977): 4–32.

———. "The Lushootseed Language Project." In *Language Renewal among American Indian Tribes: Issue, Problems, and Prospects,* ed. Robert St. Clair and William Leap, 71–89. Rossyln, Va.: National Clearinghouse for Bilingual Education, 1982.

Peter, Susie Sampson. *x̌əčusədəʔ ʔə gʷəqʷulcəʔ: Aunt Susie Sampson Peter; The Wisdom of a Skagit Elder.* Transcribed by Vi (taqʷšəblu) Hilbert, translated by Vi Hilbert and Jay Miller, recorded by Leon Metcalf. Text in Salish and English. Seattle: Lushootseed Press, 1995.

Sharing Legends at Upper Skagit. Video recording of Indian tellers from seven tribes (Upper Skagit, Tulalip, Suquamish, Sauk-Siuattle, Nooksack, Swinomish, Lummi) share legends from their tribes. Producer Crisca Bierwert Russell, director Pila Lauronel, organizer Vi Hilbert. Seattle, Wash.: Lushootseed Research, 1985.

Shelton, Ruth Sehome. *Xǝcusǝdǝ ǝ siastǝnu: The Wisdom of a Tulalip Elder; Gram Ruth Sehome Shelton.* Transcribed by Vi (taqʷšǝblu) Hilbert, translated by Vi (taqʷšǝblu) Hilbert and Jay Miller, recorded by Leon Metcalf. Seattle, Wash.: Lushootseed Press, 1995. Text in Salish and English.

Waterman, Thomas Talbot. *Puget Sound Geography.* Original manuscript by T. T. Waterman (b. 1885). Edited with additional comments by Vi Hilbert, Jay Miller, and Zalmai Zahir. Federal Way, Wash: Lushootseed Press, 2001.

About Vi (taqʷšǝblu) Hilbert

Floating Eagle Feather. "Vi Hilbert-Taqseblu: Skagit-Salish Elder, Teacher of Lushootseed Language." Interview in *Daughters of Fearlessness: A Medicine Bundle of Interviews with Spiritual Activitists,* 11–14. Newtown, New South Wales: Friends of Unicef and Greenpeace, n.d.

Huchoosedah: Traditions of the Heart. Video recording. Documentary on the life of Native American teller Vi Hilbert. Some storytelling segments. Useful portrayal of storytelling as part of the life of a culture. Seattle: KCTS-9, 1995.

Simms, Laura. "A Voiceless Blowing Sound." *Parabola: Myth, Tradition, and the Search for Meaning* 25(3) (Fall 2000): 65–73.

Yoder, Janet. *dxʷʔal taqʷšǝblu tuł ʔalti syǝyaʔyaʔs: Writings about Vi Hilbert, by Her Friends.* [Seattle]: Lushootseed Research, 1992.

For many websites about Vi and the Lushootseed culture, see Red Cedar Circle Links, http://www.artsci.wustl.edu/~jhbauer/red_cedar_circle_links.htm.

For more information about Vi's nonprofit Lushootseed Research organization, write to Lushootseed Research, 5933 Chuckanut Drive, Bow, WA, 98232.

2

Rinjing Dorje
Tibetan Tradition

This man is dead seven hundred years ago . . .
I still read his writing!
RINJING DORJE

BACKGROUND INFORMATION ABOUT TIBET

During a long history, Tibet more or less quietly acquiesced to China's purported rule and was thus left to itself. A seventeen-point agreement was signed by the Dalai Lama in May 1951, under great pressures from Mao's China. This document made more official the Chinese position that Tibet was merely a province of China but appeared to allow Tibet local government of sorts and freedom of religion. By 1959 the Tibetan people, now feeling threatened under the Chinese hand, were actively rebelling. In response, Zhou En Lai issued a statement that their rebellion had "torn up" the seventeen-point agreement and the local government was now dissolved. Under rumors of a planned kidnapping, the Dalai Lama fled to India. In 1965 the Tibet Autonomous Region was established.[1]

In the following year, the Chinese acted as invaders and suppressed Tibetan Buddhism. Some estimate that more than six thousand temples and cultural buildings were destroyed. Many Tibetans fled to nearby Nepal and on to India. There has been an influx of Chinese settlers to former Tibetan territories. Eastern Tibet in particular is said to now have two (or even three according to some estimates) Chinese to one Tibetan.[2]

Rinjing Dorje. Photo courtesy of Rinjing Dorje.

Our teller, Rinjing, lived in a Tibetan village not far from Nepal's border. His family already had ties with Nepal, including a nunnery under their patronage. So, moving to Nepal was a logical step for their family.

Meet Rinjing Dorje

Rinjing Dorje was born in 1949 in the tiny Shabru village in Tibet, about half a day's walk from the Nepalese border. His family history resembles a folktale. Rinjing's father, Sherab Dorje, was a healer. The king of Nepal's daughter was very ill. Many had tried to heal her, but all had failed. Sherab Dorje offered to take the case. Using his shamanic powers, he focused her mind by working in a darkened room and concentrating her thoughts on a single candle flame. He counseled her. He walked on her back, imparting healing. The girl was cured. As a reward, Sherab Dorje was made head of a nine-district region in the Tsun area of northern Nepal. He traveled widely in those days, acting as judge and administrator for the area. During this time, he arranged for a monastery to be built. When Rinjing's father died, his mother went to Nepal and presided over the monastery. Now that she has passed away, Rinjing's cousin oversees the monastery.

Rinjing's mother was of a herding people. They spent the winters in stone houses in the valley and climbed the mountain slopes each summer with their yaks, sheep, and cows. There they lived in tents and gathered around bonfires to socialize. It was here that Rinjing heard many of the stories he still recounts today.

When Rinjing was eleven, he became very ill. His father brought a famous astrologer who predicted that Rinjing would certainly die unless he was ordained as a monk. The lengthy rites were performed for Rinjing, who was lying all the while in his sickbed, near death's door. The next day he began to recover, and when he was well enough, he went to live at the Muen Monastery. However, life was soon disrupted again. Rinjing's father passed away, and the Chinese arrived. Rinjing was living in a monastery at the time. In 1960 he fled to Nepal along with the other monks and villagers. There Rinjing, who was now thirteen, resided at the Korwa Monastery in Kathmandu, and his mother took over responsibilities at his father's much smaller monastery, Dharma Chakra.

As he matured, Rinjing made the decision to leave the monastery. He traveled to the United States, returned to Nepal, married, and then moved permanently to the United States. He lives now in Seattle, where he earns his living as a bartender, a profession that allows ample room for Rinjing's storytelling talents. He writes industriously and has published two books. He is especially proud of his novel, *Renegade Monk*, an imaginative tale of Tibetan adventure that, he reveals, is partly autobiographical.

Talking with Rinjing

I was fortunate to have tapes of tales and commentary from Rinjing's workshops at the 1993 National Association for the Preservation and Perpetuation of Storytelling (NAPPS) conference in Seattle and tapes of the 1988 Traditional Tellers Retreat. I also was able to query Rinjing without benefit of tape, during an elegant Tibetan dinner party provided by Rinjing at the home of his friend, Tom Strickland, in Edmonds, Washington, in 1995. To fill gaps in my data, Rinjing invited me to his Edmonds apartment one fall evening in 1998 and provided a Tibetan dinner.

When we arrived at Rinjing's apartment, he had a delicious hot meal simmering on the stove for us. A friend, Joe O'Donell, came along to help provide a better audience for Rinjing's stories. We enjoyed stir-fry and rice and sipped hot tea as we talked. On the wall beside a photo of the Dalai Lama hung an amazing photograph of Rinjing's father in shamanic dress. Rinjing also brought out an old photograph of an innocent-looking teen in monk's clothing—Rinjing as a young monk. Over the couch hung a woven *tanka*, an object important in Tibetan religious storytelling traditions.

When I asked Rinjing about storytellers he had heard as a youth, he spoke of the lama mani *who traveled from town to town as professional storytellers.*
    Lama mani.
    These are regular folks. Sometimes they have families . . . they travel.
    This is not something that you go and learn from. It is like an inherited profession. They don't have a really established place where they live and so they always travel.
    And they are pretty wealthy too sometimes. They don't have a set fee but people offer them, if they are really good at it. Mostly husband and wife come. Usually woman played the music. The man recites. And they usually bring a *tanka* like that painting. (*points to the tanka hanging on his wall*) That has all pictures of different legends or stories. The man who would tell *lama mani* has a long beard, and a long metal . . . almost like a rod. It's got

all decorations on that and he chants and points to these different pictures, what they represent and all. So all the children, the whole entire villagers surround this man and he recites. So that's the *lama mani*.

Joe asks, Is that tradition continuing now?
I don't think so. *Lama mani* . . . people don't even know, young kids.
Kind of sad. That's one of the reasons I want to tell stories from Tibet . . . is to keep up that tradition. That's one of the major reasons. Because today kids, like twenty-five to thirty-six years old. They were born in India . . . or in Nepal or in foreign countries. They speak more foreign language than Tibetan. They have no knowledge of telling stories.
Like tales of Uncle Tompa . . . you just mention his *name* to Tibetans, older Tibetans in Tibet, for example. Just lama, monk, anyone. Just mention his name . . . Uncle Tompa . . . *Agu Tompa* . . . and everybody had broad smiles. Because everybody knows his stories. Because he is so popular. He's like the poor man's hero. He's after the rich and famous . . . religious leaders that prey on the poor. He has hundreds of stories. I couldn't write them all into English, because they didn't make any sense. Because of cultural difference.
Some of the *American* stories you tell them in *Tibetan* . . . they don't make any sense. You tell them in Tibetan. And some of the Tibetan stories you tell in English . . . no one can figure out what it's all about. Because there is a gap between the cultures. They see things differently.

The Drunk Sets His Beard on Fire

Rinjing gives an example of cultural confusion in storytelling.
When I was working in a bar, this one guy, drunk guy, set his *beard* on fire.
I wouldn't serve him any drinks. He was *drunk*.
And he was protesting by setting his beard on fire.
(*Rinjing is laughing*)
I went to Nepal . . . I was doing some research for my novel.
And old friends of mine . . . monks . . . I used to be a monk, one time.
The old friends they all came and greeted me, like that.
They asked me what I do.
I said, "I am a bartender. I pour drinks for people."
No one can figure out why Americans would *pay* someone to pour their drink.

(*laughs*)
In Nepal it's not done like that.
Everybody pours their own drink.
They don't have too many kinds anyway.
So then I start talking about this guy setting his beard on fire.
And I thought all these people were going to laugh you know . . .
all my friends . . . all my old friends . . .
But they all looked serious . . . sad . . .
One guy shook his head, "*Tch* . . . *tch* . . . *tch* . . ."
That means . . . *sad.*
I asked, "Isn't this funny?"
He said, "No. It's not funny."
He said, "Did you say any prayers?"
I said, "Prayer for what?"
"Oh the *fleas and ticks* . . . may have died in the fire."
There is a big cultural gap.
A *huge* gap . . . in it.

Tsten Wanggyal

I ask again about tellers Rinjing heard as a child.

The *lama mani,* and the older people in the village. They were the best storytellers . . . the older people. And there was one particularly . . . one old man, his name was Tseten Wanggyal. He was a goldsmith. That's what he did for a living.

But his . . . joy of his life was telling stories . . . telling Uncle Tompa stories.

He told the nastiest jokes I have ever heard. He liked those the most. The kids and everybody seemed to like those the most. So he was always the storyteller there.

I learned a lot from him too. A lot of the tales of Uncle Tompa that I wrote in the book they came from him.

Would you go to his house or . . .

Well we were like a big family . . . in Tibet. The villagers are all like one whole family. Everybody knows each other. You can walk into anybody's house any time you want. You don't have to knock on the door . . . just go in. And that's the kind of relationship we had.

And would he be telling them to just you?

No no . . . whole bunch of kids. He's got to have people laughing at him, otherwise he won't *like* it. (*Rinjing laughs*) He did a lot of laughing at his own jokes. He laughed at his own jokes all the time. So the kids can't stand it without laughing with him.

He was a traveling goldsmith. So he traveled village to village doing his goldsmith art. So people would pay high price to have him make earrings. He also did silver work. He also had a shop at his home, but mostly he travels. He had a wife. He goes away for a month or so and then he comes back.

So every time he came back he came back with new stories?
Yeah. He liked mostly the *nasty* stories.

So could the kids hear those?
The kids loved it.

And that's okay? The parents don't get mad?
No that's okay. Not like in America. In America you've got to be careful what you storytell.

Zhangpo

Rinjing tells about another teller in his childhood village.
Olden days, this village I grew up, Shabru, they had chiefs, like village chiefs. These chiefs, not elected, but people kind of make him chief. One chief, that I hardly remember, I was very young when he died. He was a very very kind man.

Was a very good chief. And I remember he wore a special earring. Tibetan men wear one earring on the right ear. And he had one earring it came down all the way to here. Round and long one. And in between it was embossed with a certain kind of turquoise. And it was his trademark or insignia of being a chief. He was a baldheaded old man. Wrinkled, beautiful smile. He always told stories. He was a storyteller also.

And . . . his name was Zhangpo. My mother told me . . . I don't remember . . . my mother told me that he . . . every morning . . . we lived by the hills . . . little valley. He would go up in the top of the hill and look down at the village. Make sure every home had smoke coming out of the house . . . for breakfast. If there was a house with no smoke coming out he would send somebody to look and see why somebody is making no food. So that was his tradition of looking after his village.

He will go out . . . look around . . . make sure everybody has breakfast smoke coming out. If not, he will go there himself or send other family members . . . make sure why everybody is not eating. If the family lacks some food or something, they all put together and try to help the family. So that was his nature. But I don't remember him very well. That was what my mother told me. He was a great storyteller too.

When he was telling stories I was very little . . . maybe five or six. The only thing I remember was his long earring. I remember him telling stories but I don't remember what he told. Lot of times he told god stories . . . deities and goddesses of the mountains . . . and always outside . . . at the bonfire where kids sit around the fire. He had a big . . . this one particular area . . . in the summertime up in the mountains.

He would sit on this big rock . . . where he always sat. He walks around with a gourd . . . filled with *chee* . . . some kind of *chee*. He sits there . . . he sits on this rock and tells the stories . . . and the children sitting around listening to him. I wish I had been a little older.

Did he use gestures?

A lot of gestures . . . facial expressions . . . Sometimes he would stand up and start moving his body a little like that.

Would he change his voice?

Yeah, he would change his voice too. The kids all liked him.

Why Rinjing Tells Stories

I asked Rinjing why he tells stories.

I just read a phrase by an American writer, Isaac Singer. That really kind of inspired me. He said that "What happened to you yesterday was a story for today. Today, what happened today was a story for tomorrow. If the stories weren't told and the books weren't written . . . we would live like animals." That was an inspiration to me.

So I tell like . . . stories should be told. And my phrase is . . . my motto is, "Life is a story. And no two stories are alike."

So I feel like stories must be told. It's just like a shadow . . . just follows you. Once you die, the shadow is no longer there. So nothing is left behind. Rabindranath Tagore said, "When you die, you take with you what you do to yourself. You leave behind, what you do to others." And those kind of things . . . that really made me tell stories. What I do to other people . . . maybe I die many years later. People will say, "This guy was a storyteller." They will remember it.

Rinjing's Story of Deciding to Become a Writer

When I decided I wanted to be a writer, that was when I was in the monastery, eleven or twelve years old.

We had a big library in the monastery.

And the young monks were sent in there to study.

And I was reading this old commentary.

And the books were not like this.

The books were wood carved.

And printed on the wood carved.

This book had like six hundred pages.

It was a commentary by a fellow by the name of *Rinjing Dorje.*

And I looked at the date.

That was like *seven hundred years ago* he wrote that book.

I was going . . . oooohhhh. I was going . . . WOW!

This man is dead seven hundred years ago . . . I still read his writing!

That was my strongest force that I found.

I wanted to be a writer like him.

Because he had the same name as me.

That really inspired me actually.

That made me want to be a writer.

And today I still pursue it.

I can't make a living.

But I can still try it.

Entering the World of Professional Storytelling

Rinjing first entered the world of professional storytelling in 1988 when he spoke at our Traditional Tellers Retreat. A Seattle Storyteller's Guild board member, Martha Smith, was a friend of Rinjing and told of hearing him tell marvelous tales over dinner. Rinjing says he was always thought of as a great storyteller, even back in Nepal. Friends would come over and encourage him to tell his funny stories. His *Tales of Uncle Tompa* (1977) had been published in 1977. The extremely bawdy nature of the tales, however, limited the market for the book. His *Food in Tibetan Life* (Prospect Books, 1985) also includes some tale material. Recently, Rinjing has begun to take the notion of professional storytelling in the United States seriously. He is working on his performance skills and is taking steps to shape a repertoire that is more acceptable to American audiences. Some of his favorite stories are just too bawdy for even adult audiences in the United States. He now tells personal stories, mostly humorous anecdotes, some of the less scatological Uncle Tompa trickster stories, and Jataka stories from his Tibetan Buddhist background. His jolly irreverence occasionally runs him afoul of those westerners who expect a former Tibetan monk to possess a certain holy aura.

The Aura of the Teller

I was up in Vancouver . . . few years back . . . to tell stories.
This was a group of . . . westerners they follow Buddhism.
I'm not much of a Buddhist . . . Buddhist storyteller.
I tell Jataka stories, that's about it.
They invited me there.
It was the late in the evening.
It was so dark. It was raining, raining . . .
I couldn't find it, this place. Took me a long time.
I had this little Volkswagen.
I was driving, driving. Trying to find this place.
When I finally got there . . .
the people started bowing!
Like I was a high monk or something.
I said, "No, I am just an ordinary storyteller. I am nothing special."
One lady said, "Oh we saw your aura coming out.
The rain and your aura.
When you were coming down."
"Aura for me? No, I don't think I have aura."
"Yeah! We saw your *aura!*" these two ladies.
"Ohhh I think that was my *headlights.*"
(*We all crack up laughing at this.*)
That was my Volkswagen headlights. Not my aura.
They were insisting it was my aura.
I didn't know what to say.
I *know* I don't have aura.
They had already made up their mind what I should be.

Rinjing's Tales

THE SOUP

One of my favorite Rinjing stories is this personal account from his days as a
young monk. I have asked him to tell the story of the soup.

The soup!

I was a lowly cook.

Nothing special. Just a monk.

And I was assigned to do kitchen work . . . cooking.

I learned a lot of cooking there too.

This monastery had about forty-five monks.

Every year . . . during the Buddha's birthday.

Sixteen days . . . during May . . . that's the month that Buddha was
    born . . .

the monks go on fasting . . . for sixteen days.

Must stop eating sixteen days.

Every other day . . . you can eat a big large meal.

The next day you don't eat anything.

Not only you don't eat anything. You can't drink anything.

And you can't *talk*. No conversations.

But next day . . . you can eat one meal. But it has to be exactly at noon.

But no meat, no spices, no garlic . . . nothing.

Just vegetables and beans and rice and things like that.

And you have to eat at noon. Other words, if you pass noon, then you
    can't eat.

Then the next day you don't eat again.

It alternates.

And I was in the kitchen one day.

This big pot of soup we were boiling.

Dumpling soup. All kinds of carrots, beans, vegetables, everything else.

Big pot of soup . . . for the noon that day.

And all the monks come with their wooden bowls.

They were very hungry. Because they hadn't eaten the day before.

So right at noon.

You pick it up and you set it in the middle.

And they will help themselves with their wooden bowls.

There are like six, seven ladles.

This particular day . . . this one, Hotpa, this guy's name . . . he was the
  chef.
He said, "Rinjing. You pick up . . . and set in the middle."
So I was like . . . at that time I was about seventeen years old.
I picked up the pot . . . big pot.
Those monks were waiting, they were hungry . . . ready to eat.
I picked up the pot . . . and it didn't have any handles.
I was bringing like this . . . all of a sudden it slipped right out of my hands!
(*laughs*)
Spatter all over the floor!
Not a drop of soup in the pot.
Oh boy! Those monks were *mad!*
They starved the whole day.
Now they can't eat next day. Past noon. No food.
I had to run away from there.
I thought they were going to hit me.
They were *really* mad.

Later they had to bring a whole pack of street dogs . . . to lick it up.
The monks didn't eat all day now. *Two* days now.
That's the one story I was telling Martha. She really liked that.
Tellin' about pissed off monks.

Joe: I thought they were peaceful.
  Not when it comes to food!

UNCLE TOMPA GETS A *MOMO*

*One of Rinjing's favorites is the story of Uncle Tompa tricking his teacher at the
monastery. Rinjing says he likes these stories because they show that the monks
are ordinary people, with feelings and foibles like anyone else.*
  One day Uncle Tompa decided he wanted to go visit his parents.
  His parents were not very wealthy and he went to visit them and that was
not much fun for him.
  And a few days later he came back.
  He walked into the monastery. Into the room where his guru lived.
  And he smelled something.
  He smelled some *momos* [a boiled meat pastry].
  He was quite hungry and he hadn't eaten all day.
  But in Tibet it is impolite to ask, "Can I share your food?"

It is quite impolite.

He looked in and there was his guru having a big plate full of *momos*.

He thought, "I'd like to get some of that. I don't know how to ask him."

He walked in and said, "Gela! Gela! I am back!"

The master looked up. "Are you back? Good."

He kept eating his *momos*.

So Uncle Tompa sat right next to him and said, "You know what Gela? I found a big bag full of gold."

Well that really drew some interest from his guru.

"What happened?"

And he gave one *momo* to Uncle Tompa.

He popped it in his mouth and he ate.

Then he said, "Well, I took the bag to my parents.

And I told them I was going to take this bag full of gold to my teacher."

The guru became even more interested.

He gave him another *momo*. And he ate that.

"What happened then?"

"They wanted half for themselves."

"So what happened then?" The guru gave him another *momo* . . . a third *momo*.

"But I told them I live with my guru and I have to take this gold to my guru."

So he became *more* interested. He gave him another *momo*.

This went on for some time.

Then he noticed that there were no more *momos* left on the plate.

So the teacher kept asking, "What happened?"

So he stretched his arms . . .

gently rubbed his eyes . . .

"Then I woke up."

After the audience has laughed, Rinjing adds . . .

That tells of the nonattachment beliefs of Tibetan Buddhism!

HOT *MOMO!*

Rinjing has a true story about a monk and momo.

In my village there was a very high exalted lama was traveling through and he happened to be my father's friend. Old friend from his village. So he stayed at our house. He had been traveling for days and days and he and his attendant stayed at our house. And that evening my mother made some *momos*. *Momos* are the most special gift you can prepare for a guest. A meat dumpling. This lama was very hungry. He was sitting there. In Tibet we don't say, "I'm hungry." That would be very impolite. He had hot tea, and waiting for the meal. And my father had invited a bunch of village kids there . . . like ten or twelve kids and grownups. And we were all sitting there facing him. He was facing down from his seat.

My mother suddenly brings a big plate of *momos*. These *momos* are steamed, like steam dumplings. Usually eat them steamed, that is good enough. But to make them really special . . . you fried them in hot oil after they are steamed. So she had them all deep-fried. And big plate full of that and then hot sauce on the side and then some other vegetables for the lama. And the lama was very hungry. We were all looking up this way and he was sitting up there . . . and he did his prayers . . . said his prayers. And he picked up the one *momo* . . . that was deep fried . . . and he popped it right in his mouth. He didn't realize it just came out of the oil! It sounded like a frying pan. It went "Sssssss." Right in his mouth!

And in Tibet it is really impolite to spit it out. So he held it in his mouth . . . tears rolling down. We don't drink cold water. Everything is hot . . . hot tea . . . hot sauce . . .

He held it in his mouth and it was sizzling . . . frying pan . . . ssssss.

And everybody heard it. But it was impolite to laugh. You were supposed to keep quiet. All the kids, we all heard it. The whole entire audience heard.

And after he left, next day, my father was scolding my mom . . . "Why did you bring such hot *momos*? His mouth is *fried* now."

UNCLE TOMPA WORKS AS A PORTER

Uncle Tompa always was poor. He was always running out of food or something.

And one day he decided to go to Lhasa.

So he took a big rope.

He wanted to become a . . . get a job with somebody in the village.

So he sat around with some other porters, waiting for somebody to come by.

So he squatted. Wait . . . wait . . . wait . . .

No customers. Nobody wants porters.

Keep waiting . . .

All of a sudden . . . there was a guy came in . . . dressed rich.

Said . . . "Hey porter!"

"Yeah?"

"I have a big box of china that I just bought.

I want someone to carry this to my house."

But the guy was really sly.

Says, "I don't wanna pay you guys in money.

But in return I will give you three pieces of advice.

For the service . . . you can carry this box to my house."

And all these other porters.

"No . . . we don't want to . . ." They shook their heads.

"No . . . we need money."

Course Uncle Tompa thought . . .

"Something like *money* I can earn anytime I want.

But good advice . . . is hard to come by.

This guy going to give me three good advices."

So Uncle Tompa says, "OK. I will carry your box."

"OK."

So Uncle Tompa goes . . . and picks up this heavy big box . . .

full of china . . . he just bought.

In Tibet we have no cars. You have to walk everywhere you go.

So he ties the rope around and carries on his back.

And walked and walked.

He lived up in the hills.

He walks a distance.

And Uncle Tompa carrying this . . . and . . .

"You told me you were going to give me three pieces of advice.

Would you give me one now?"

The rich man looked at him.

Said, "Yeah. Here is your first advice.

Do not believe anyone who tells you not better to keep a full stomach than to go hungry."

And Uncle Tompa looked at him. "Yeah, okay.

That's your first advice."

So he goes on.

Walks and walks . . . another mile or so.

Uncle Tompa is sweating and all that . . . so heavy.

Says, "What about my second advice now?"

The man says, "Do not believe anyone who tells you better to walk on foot than ride a horse."

"Ahh. Okay.

Not too bad."

Keep walk and walk and walk.

They came to the big man's house.

Where he entered the door.
Uncle Tompa still sweating and tired . . . panting.
"How about my third and last one?"
"Do not believe anyone who tells you they are a fool like you."
Uncle Tompa let go of his rope and . . . *bam!* Dropped the whole box.
On the floor. Shattered every china he had in the box.

He looked at the man and he said.
"Do not believe anyone who tells you that none of your china is broken."
(*laughs*)
So he walked away.
That was the end.

EATING THE POISON

Again he was poor.
And one day the regional governor hired him to go with him as a servant.
So he carried a big load of his pots and pans.
This regional guy, this official was going to Lhasa.
So he was riding a horse.
And while Uncle Tompa carried a heavy load in the back and walked.
And this guy was so mean and stingy to Uncle Tompa, even though he
    was working so hard for him.
He ate all the good food.
Uncle Tompa was left just the leftovers or some crappy food he brought
    to feed the servant.
He went on, days go by, several days and they finally came to Lhasa.
The official he had to go to some kind of meeting.
So Uncle Tompa stayed in his house . . . they rented.
And he told . . . there was a bag full of *tsampa*. It's a Tibetan staple, a
    Tibetan food.
It is a flour . . . roasted barley flour . . . we call it *tsampa* . . . we eat like rice.
In Tibet we can't grow rice so we eat *tsampa*.
And he had especially fine quality *tsampa* in his bag.
So before the official left, he told Uncle Tompa.
"Hey. Uncle Tompa. Don't eat the *tsampa*.
Because this is all poison. If you eat it, you will die."
And eggs . . . are very expensive in Tibet.
We don't get much eggs. Eggs are very rare.
So there was a pot full of boiled eggs and he put a lid on.

He said, "Uncle Tompa, don't open up this lid.
There are birds in there.
If you open it they will all fly away if you open it."
And Uncle Tompa, he was very smart.
He pretend like . . . "Oh no, I won't open.
I won't eat *tsampa*."
As soon as he left, he ate all the *tsampa*. He knew it was not poison.
He ate all the eggs.
And he had a good meal for the first time.
And that night the official came back.
Uncle Tompa pretended like he was all cringing . . . shaking from fear.
Said, "What happened?"
"Oh . . . those birds were making so much noise . . .
I opened up the lid just a little bit and *all* the birds flew *away* . . . from
   your pot.
I was so scared . . . of how you were going to do me harm . . .
So I decided to kill myself . . .
from eating the poisonous *tsampa*.
So I ate all the *tsampa*.
But I still didn't die.
So that was the end. But he got even with *him*.

MOVING THE BIG ROCK

So he ran out of food.
And in that region, in the village . . . that region . . . there was a very rich
   man.
He had many farms . . . many fields . . .
and one of those fields had a big boulder sticking in the middle.
And he wanted to see if he could talk him into giving him some food . . .
   but it won't be very easy . . . I'm going to trick him.
So he goes to the rich man's house.
"Hey, Landlord."
"Yeah."
"Why don't you remove that big boulder.
It's taking so much space of your rich field.
You should take that away . . . move that away."
He said, "It's so big. Who can take that out?"
He said, "Ahhh. That's no problem. I can carry it."
It was *huge* . . . about the size of a house!

Huge boulder and . . . "I can carry it."

Rich man, "You can?"

"Yeah.

But you've got to hire about twenty-five strong able-bodied men who can
    push it so I can carry it on my back."

So . . . "Twenty-five people? Yeah, I can hire them. Yeah, okay that's fine."

So he shows up early the next morning.

So he has his breakfast . . . at the rich man's.

He waited and keep talking to him . . . talking to him.

And finally the twenty-five strong men show up.

They are supposed to be pushing the strong rock on his back so he can
    carry it.

He keeps talking to the rich man.

"Oh . . . it's almost noon anyway.

I might as well have my lunch."

So he gave him his lunch.

And he ate the lunch.

And they kept talking and talking.

And later on, it started getting afternoon.

"Uncle Tompa . . . those people are waiting out there.

You want to go?"

"Well I'll have my dinner now."

So he gave him his dinner.

"I'll go all in one trip. I'll go there . . .

It's so easy.

As long as they can push it on my back . . . load it on my back . . .

I can carry so easy."

The rich man's livid.

But pretty soon he says,

"Uhhh. Might also give me my wages too today.

So I don't have to come back and bother you."

So the Rich Man gives him the money . . . to carry the rock . . .

Charges enormous amount of money.

So he goes there . . . slowly goes down . . . he's all full . . . eaten all day . . .
and got some money now.

So he puts a rope around this big huge boulder . . .

and he leans against the boulder like this . . .

Then he shouts to these guys . . . twenty-five people out there . . .

"Push . . . push . . .

Push . . . push! . . ."

They push. And not even a slight inch can be moved. It was such a big
  rock.
"Hey come on . . . push . . . push . . ." He shouted several more times.
They couldn't push . . . move it even inches.
They gave up.
He took the rope from around.
Went in to the rich man.
Said, "These people are too *weak*.
They can't even load it on my back.
If they had loaded it on my back I could have moved.
So I can't. It's *their* fault I can't move it.
So he walked away from there.
(*laughed*)
That's the one boulder story.
I like that too.

Notes

1. www.tibetinfo.net/news-updates/nu210501.htm#HB.
2. www.savetibet.org.

Bibliography

Dorje, Rinjing. *Food in Tibetan Life*. Illustrated by the author. Tibetan script by Venera-
  ble T. G. Dhongthong. London: Prospect Books, 1985.
———. *The Renegade Monk of Tibet*. Edmonds, Wash.: Banyan Press, 2005.
———. *Tales of Uncle Tompa: The Legendary Rascal of Tibet*. Illustrations by Addison
  Smith. New York: Barrytown, Ltd., and Station Hill Arts, 1977.

For information about Rinjing and his Banyan Press, see www.thetibetanstoryteller.com
and www.bayanpress.com.

Roberto Carlos Ramos. Photo courtesy of Fernando Giulia.

3

Roberto Carlos Ramos
The Power of Words

I discovered the power that words could have over me, and over other people.
Roberto Carlos Ramos

Background Information about Belo Horizonte, Brazil

Belo Horizonte is the capital of the Brazilian state of Minas Gerais and is the third largest city in Brazil. The 2003 population was approximately 2.35 million. This beautiful city is graced with parks, historic churches, and contemporary art centers set amid a sea of high-rise buildings.[1]

Belo Horizonte was chosen by the United Nations Population Crisis Committee as the city with the best quality of life in Latin America. The city is proud of its architecture, including the Pampulha complex with various projects by Oscar Niemeyer.

Belo Horizonte is located in a region of many natural wonders—lakes, mountains, rivers, and caves. Even within city limits, there are 32 square meters of green space per inhabitant.[2] Belo Horizonte is surrounded by slopes of the Serra do Curral. The city is about 250 miles inland from Rio de Janeiro, abutting on some of the last remaining coastal rain forest in Brazil. For photos of this lively city, see http://www.belohorizonte.mg.gov.br/por/index.php.

Meet Roberto Carlos Ramos

Roberto Carlos Ramos was left at an orphanage by his parents when he was five years old. The poor family had ten children and believed they could help their young son by turning him over to the state. The child was miserable. He refused to obey or to learn. By the time he was thirteen, he had run away 132 times! At this point his life took a remarkable turn. A French social worker, who was living in Belo Horizonte at the time, saw hope in this wayward street child and took him into her home. Roberto Carlos will tell you the rest of his story.

I met Roberto Carlos while telling at a massive Tellabration event in Rio in 1998. Roberto Carlos was far and away the star of our show, which included teller after teller in an afternoon-long performance. His ability to draw the audience to him like a magnet was remarkable. I recall that a cute young TV reporter was attempting to interview children *while* he was telling. The TV star and her camera crew were totally ignored by the kids as they leaned away to keep all eyes on Roberto Carlos and not miss a word of his story. Later Roberto Carlos was a part of our 2001 King County Library System Storyfest International. Though he told in Portuguese, his animation was so strong that folks remembered him as having spoken English! Livia de Almeida translated for Roberto Carlos in a fluid performance that let nothing fall through the cracks. But once Roberto Carlos got on a roll, translation was hardly necessary!

Talking with Roberto Carlos

For the most part, Livia de Almeida translated while I talked with Roberto Carlos, though some communication was in English and some in my bastardized Spanish.[3] Our most extensive interview took place around the table after dinner at our Guemes Island home. There my daughter Jennifer and her husband Nat provided an eager audience for Roberto Carlos. The story texts were transcribed from performance tapes of Roberto Carlos telling at the Bothell, Bellingham, Lake Hills, and Burien libraries during his July 1999 visit.

Telling Tales at an Early Age

I asked Roberto Carlos when he began telling stories.
    When I was about eight years old.

I didn't know how to read or write.
My friends and I didn't know how to read or write.
And I had already run away *twelve* times from the institution where I
    lived.
And I felt a great necessity of knowing information about the world.

We would listen to what the adults were talking about.
Even if it wasn't a very interesting subject, we would be listening.
I learned something very soon.
The good storyteller was the one who told the tales people really wanted
    to hear.
The stories that the people *want* to hear.
I realized that my friends liked to listen to news about kidnappings, rob-
    beries, and accidents, car crashes.
Because in the streets they saw this kind of stuff.

But it was one thing to live these kinds of situations . . .
the other was to listen to *stories* about things like that.
And they were tales . . . not real.
So I would pick up the newspaper on the newsstand.
And start . . . pretending to be reading it to my friends.
I usually created things that surprised myself!
I would tell stories about trains . . . that ran over people fourteen times.
Children who would fall from sixteen-floor buildings without getting hurt.
What really mattered was not just giving that information to my friends . . .
but telling stories as if they were true . . . and they were facts.
And I tried to express that with my body and with my face, exactly as if I
    were reading a newspaper.
And then they believed what I read.
And they asked me to read.
I presented it as if I was reading.
Well there was always the risk of somebody else, who knew how to read,
to say that I *couldn't* read.
Sometimes people who knew how to read, they would read carelessly,
they would read, repeating words and stumbling over words . . .
without expressing or intonation.
So the boys would think that the person who knew how to read wasn't
    reading at all . . .
that *I* could read much better than that person.
They were sure that *I* knew how to read.

And the other person that could really read,
they wouldn't believe it because he lacked expression.

I always wanted to learn, very much, how to read and write.
When I was nine I even asked to come back to the orphanage ... institu-
tion ...
to learn how to read and write. To be able to read and write.
But they always said that I wouldn't stay there, that I would run away.
I had to go to another school. To a school outside the institution.
I asked not to be identified as a boy from the institution.
But it was exactly the same as before.
The first thing that happened when I got there at the new school.
*Roberto Carlos continued to run away from the orphanage. He did not learn to
read until he was in his teens.*

Sahita Guides Roberto Carlos

Who did you hear stories from as a child?
When I was nine years old, I was moved from one institution, which was
downtown in the city, to an institution which was in the countryside.
And there we had a cook.
The cook of the orphanage, she would tell tales to me.
She was black.
She didn't know how to read or write.
But she would tell many tales about the popes and about history.
She said that when Brazil was discovered by Cabral, five hundred years
ago ...
she was there by the beach, selling meat dumplings to the Portuguese.
And people would confirm the thing that she had told.
And they would say, "Yes, yes. Brazil was reached by Cabral.
And he was looking for the way to India." And so ... well this is truth
then.
For the first time, I had a good feeling about myself.

*Roberto Carlos revealed that before this he wanted so badly to be on a local
children's television program. He watched it and thought how wonderful it
would be to be on that program. But all the boys on the program were blond.
He refers to this as his "existential crisis."*
This cook was the first person I met who was black, and she seemed to be
happy to be black, and she was full of happiness with being black. And I was

thinking, "How could she possibly be so happy with being black?" Once when I was playing with her, I said something that was very common in Brazil to say. I said that she was a black woman with a white soul. In that age when you wanted to praise a black man, you would say that he had a white soul. And when I said that to her, she wouldn't say anything. She said that one day I would be proud to be a black man.

And she was the first one who touched me on this point of being black . . . and being proud.

When I was about ten . . .

I had already run away many times.

I talked to the woman and told her I didn't like the way my life was turning.

That's when she talked to me and told me she knew a thing . . . which could change people's lives.

She looked at me and said that she knew of a kind of tea . . .

A tea that could change people's lives.

I asked what kind of tea is that?

She said it was a secret recipe.

Few people knew how to make it.

And she told me that each person had a different leaf which was good for him,

which could make his kind of tea.

I looked at her. And I realized that she wasn't lying.

She was telling me the truth.

So I begged her to make me that tea.

She said that one day she would make that tea for me.

And I kept pestering her and asking her to make the tea for me.

But she always said that I would have to come back later.

One day I was on the roof.

I had run away. I was bored and mad.

I wanted to do something bad. So I would be sent to another orphanage again.

I was throwing pieces of the tile from the roof.

She was down on the ground and she looked at me.

She said it was time to make the tea.

I climbed down from the roof and she told me that I would have to go to pick the tea at her house.

I walked to her house to pick the leaf.

I saw a wood stove in her house.
She would make the tea on this wood stove.
She brewed some of the tea on her stove.
And she asked me to drink the tea.
She told me I had to swallow the tea in three gulps.
Always thinking of the things I wanted for my own life.
The first thing I thought . . . I want to be blond.
Second . . . I would like to be powerful as a judge.
Third . . . I wanted to live in a castle.
I wanted to be king.

I thought it would work immediately.
But she claimed that it wouldn't work immediately.
The tea was like a seed. It needed time to work.
She told me that if I wanted it to work . . .
I had to observe the people I wanted to become like.
If I wanted to become blond . . .
I had to observe blond people, how they acted.
Because then when I became blond, I would know how to act as a blond
    person.
If I wanted to be powerful like a judge . . .
I had to observe how powerful people acted.
If I wanted to be rich and live in a castle . . .
I had to observe how rich people, people who lived in castles, acted.
And for a while after that I was always looking around.

But after a few months I noticed that nothing was happening.
My hair wasn't becoming lighter.
And I started to have doubts about the tea.

After two more years, I ran away from that orphan home.
When I was thirteen years, I was living in the orphanage where I met the
    French woman.

*The social worker, Marguerite Duvas, had come to observe the orphanage
where Roberto Carlos was living. She noticed him and asked the officials about
that boy. They told her that he was incorrigible . . . a hopeless case. She told
them that no child was hopeless.*

I knew somebody was talking about me.
She came to me and she asked if she could please talk to me.
It was the first time somebody asked if they could talk to me.
As she was French, she had a very strong accent.
I told her I was worried about her speech problem.
She said, no, she didn't have a problem with her speech,
that she came from another country and where she came from every-
    body spoke the same way.
She asked about my story and seemed really interested in what I said.

Two days later I was on the street.
I had run away again.
And I met this woman.
She asked me why I had run away.
She invited me to stay for a week at her house.
Instead of staying for a week, I stayed for two months, three months . . .
The first thing, when I got inside her house,
I started looking to see what I could steal.

But after some time . . . she was so nice to me . . .
I thought, "If she sends me away . . .
I will take the stereo.
And I will leave the rest."

*Roberto Carlos taught Marguerite Duvas to understand street talk, and she
taught him to speak French. He stayed on with her and she treated him as a
son. He was especially proud of a light blue suit she had made for him.*

With that suit and walking by her side,
she was blonde and six foot tall . . .
People would say, "Oooh. Such a nice boy! Is it your son?
He looks so much like you."
I thought, "Oh good. I am really becoming blond!"

*Roberto Carlos stayed on with Marguerite Duvas and become an educated
young man. He attended college, lived for a time in France with her, and
returned to work in the same institution where he had been an orphan.
Eventually he visited his birth parents, and his mother was delighted to see
what a fine, educated man her son had become. She said it was just as the*

social worker had told her. The social worker had said that if they put their son in the orphanage, he would become an educated man and have a good career.

Roberto Carlos began to feel that the tea had actually worked. He didn't want to become blond anymore. And he did have an education, a job, and some power. He was no longer so poor as he had been.

Marguerite Duvas planned to bring Roberto Carlos back to France when he turned twenty-one. He was looking forward to that new adventure. But just before he turned twenty-one, tragedy struck and his foster mother died of an aneurism. Thus he lost in one stroke his mentor, friend, and surrogate mother.

The day I got the news about her death,
I was working at the same orphanage where I had been.
There people still made fun of me.
They called me "Dr. Black Man."

That day the gatekeeper said to me, "Do you see that guy on the street out there?"
It was a boy who used drugs, he had no way out.
The gatekeeper said, "I am not letting him come inside the orphanage.
He would make trouble. I will keep him outside."

I went to that boy.
It was raining badly.
The boy came close to me and asked for money.
I told him I had no money.
The boy asked for a cigarette.
I told him I did not smoke.
The boy wanted anything.
But I said I didn't have anything to give him.

The boy said that the worst thing to him was that when he walked the streets people ran away and were afraid of him.
I thought about what the educational theories I had been studying would say to do here.
Nothing would be of use in helping this boy.
Then I remembered the tea.

I looked at the boy.
I said, "I know of a tea which can change lives."

He thought I was making fun of him.
But I looked at him very seriously and told him that I did know of a kind
of tea which could change lives.
So I took him to my house to make him some tea.
He thought I would make it very soon.
But it took me a year to make him the tea.
He would often ask me to make that tea.
At first, I thought that the tea hadn't worked for me,
but when I began to think about it, I decided it *had* worked for me.
I didn't *want* to become blond anymore.
I was happy with myself.
Before I had been in disgrace, but now, with an education . . .
I was like a doctor or a lawyer.
And the castle? I could build my own castle.
I was healthy and I could build it.
And I realized that the tea had actually worked.
So I got on the bus and I went to the orphanage out in the country to ask
the cook how to make the tea.
When I met her, she was very frail and very old.
I asked her if she remembered me.
Maybe she had not remembered because there were so many boys there.
But she laughed and said of course she remembered me.
I told her I had come all the way out there to learn how to make this tea.
Because now I had a child who needed this kind of tea.

She had a bright smile on her face.
And suddenly I realized what it was.
She said *any* kind of leaf will do.

So I came back to my house with a leaf,
and I made the same kind of tea for this boy.
With the same seriousness which she had done.

Since then I have made tea for all my boys.

*Roberto Carlos lives now in Bairro Jardin Das Rosas in Ibirité, Belo Horizonte,
with twelve boys whom he has taken in from the streets. They worked together
to build a home that they call "The Castle."*

About Storytelling

On Using Storytelling in the Classroom

When Roberto Carlos returned from France, he began to work with youth in the same institution where he had lived as an orphan.
> And the things I had learned at the university . . .
> nothing worked when I would be inside a classroom with fourteen students.
> And when the class was through, there were only three or four in the class.
> Because the rest had run away.

> I realized that the things I was learning in the university,
> they were not working for me . . . for the boys.
> And they had not worked for *me* either when I was a student.

> And I was thinking . . . what could possibly hold their attention?
> After two months, I started to tell the story of the werewolf. (*Sahita, the cook, had told him many stories of the werewolf*)
> And I noticed that credibility, to make the story believable, was very important.
> I had brought the supernatural inside the classroom.
> And one day I told werewolf, one, two, and three.
> I had to start to *create* the story of the werewolf to hold the attention of these students.
> And then something completely different began to happen.
> I used to start the class with fourteen students and end up with two.
> Everything changed.
> After the break . . . fifteen *more* students would come to the class.
> So I realized that I could use stories
> to try to make what I wanted to do.
> From then on I started to tell stories.
> And I started to work with the stories that I remembered from my child-hood.

On Scary Tales

Roberto Carlos loves to tell "jump" tales that scare the audience. He commented on this.
> The story only wakes the things that the person already has inside.

The story doesn't make a new fear on you, a new horror.
I tell tales that make the people scared.
But the scare is not in the story.
The scare is in the person.
And the "jump" makes the person express the fear that is already inside of them.

When I tell tales, sometimes I notice that a boy who is in the audience is moving his hands nervously and is staying very close to his mother.
I can see that he is frightened.
But the story doesn't bring something new,
it is something that is already inside the boy.
And when he is listening to the story,
in a certain way he *lives* that fear.

On Gestures

I use gestures in the way I talk and the way I tell the story.
I used lots of gestures to tell my story, even when I was twelve.
Sometimes I would search for the words and couldn't find them.
Then I will use a facial expression, and my body will tell more than the words.
I would walk around sometimes and watch.
Just notice the different ways that people who tell stories would tell tales.
So I really incorporate the tricks of the people I watch.
For example, when I tell of a person telling a secret,
I look to one side and then the other, as if I am really looking to see if anybody else is listening.
So it makes the audience feel like an accomplice in the secret.
I often place my finger over my mouth, as if searching for something deep in the back of my memory.

Collecting Stories with Marguerite Duvas

I asked Roberto Carlos about others from whom he had learned folktales. He told of traveling with the Frenchwoman who took him into her home when he was fourteen. Marguerite Duvas was working in alternative education. She realized that so much was transmitted best through stories, so she was traveling around the Brazilian countryside collecting stories. And young Roberto Carlos accompanied her.

She always asked to hear the stories and later she asked me to tell the stories to her again, because she didn't understand the local dialect.
So I would hear the story, listen to the story,
and then I would repeat the story in a way she could understand.

I remember that when I used to go with Marguerite Duvas to interview
tellers in small towns, I would watch the way people acted.
Sometimes people would look at us in a distrustful way.
I use this same expression to this day when I want to show that I am not
trusting somebody in the story.
I make the same kind of face people showed to us then.

I also learned how to negotiate with people, while I was traveling with
Marguerite Duvall.
When we went inside a house, we would never ask directly for a story.
First we would accept coffee.
Then we would say that the flowers were beautiful.
Then we would say that the cake they had served was absolutely fantastic.
We would invite these people to come and visit us in our own house
someday.
Then we would tell the story of *ourselves.*
And after they felt that they were among friends, then the other person
would finally share a story with us.
Because by then we were not just any person, we were friends.

The Power of Words

When I started to tell my own life story,
I started to live lots of things that I didn't even remember were there.
And as I kept on telling my own story,
I started to discover more and more things, and to remember *little* things,
and to understand better what I had been through.
To tell the tale,
to talk about it,
helped me keep my head alive.
This time of my life when . . .
people would say I was good for *nothing*
and they would say that I was on drugs, before I did drugs.
They accused me of being a thief.
And they would say many things that I *wasn't.*

So I began to try to correspond to the image that people had of me.
So, when I was a teenager . . .
I discovered the power that words could have over me,
and over other people.

I discovered that if people used words to make me feel down,
I should use words to feel better and to help other people feel better.
Maybe it's because of that that I tell stories today.

Roberto Carlos's Stories

THE MONSTER MARAIMBAI

This is the story of a little girl about your age.[4]
She lived by herself in a little house by the forest.
She didn't have a father or a mother . . .
And the only thing she knew how to do was she made candies.
She would cook all day long.
And when they were finished,
she would put them by the kitchen window.
And then everybody would buy them.
She ended up trying to buy herself a bicycle.
The first time she saw a bicycle in her life.
she ran up to the bicycle. Eeeeehhhhh! (*excited squeal*)
And she said, "I am going to buy myself a bike!"
So she saved all her money.
But she went to the store . . .
And her money was never enough.

So she went home . . . made more candies . . .
Made more money . . .
And when she went back to the store . . .
The money was not enough.
She was almost giving up.
But then she had an idea.
And when we have an idea we make a face like that . . . "Ah-*ha!*"
"I am going to make lots and lots of candies and sell them in the *town!*"

On the first day she had made already 599 candies.

There were lots of candies on her window.
There were candies under her bed . . .
Over her table . . .
And on all her shelves.
Everybody wanted to buy the candy.
But she kept on working.

Then one night when she was working late, she heard the clock strike
twelve. Bing . . . bing . . . bing . . .
"I shouldn't be working too late.
A monster could appear."
And she heard a wind start to blow around the candy. (*wind-blowing
sounds*)
All the candies were blown around.

And when she looked at the window . . .
she saw huge hands . . . and four feet . . .
And the hands were grabbing the candies and eating them. (*gobbling
noises*)
And she thought what kind of thing is this?
It's trying to make me scared.
When it puts its hand in again . . . I am going to grab it.
When it put its hand up again . . . she jumped and "*Ahaa!*"

But the hand was cold.
And it started to shake . . .
And "AAAAHHH!" (*Roar*)
There was in front of her . . . the Maraimbai.

He had the body of a bull.
He had three arms.
A mouth that opens like that . . .
And 362 teeth!
Terrible big eyes . . .
And two horns.

And he spoke to her:
"Little girl . . . (*in scary low nasal tone*)
You are lucky . . .

I usually like to eat little girls . . .
But your candies are so good . . .
I will come every night at midnight . . .
If you don't make me candies . . .
I will swallow you."

The little girl was so frightened. (*crying sounds*)
She started making more candies.
And every night she would put her candies by her window . . .
And she heard this big noise . . .
(*stomp . . . stomp . . . stomp . . . munching noises*)
But one day there was nothing left to make candies.
There was no more sugar . . .
No more flour . . .
No more coconut . . .
She was sitting by her door.

When along came three salesmen.
The first had a basket full of needles.
"Needles! Needles! Needles for sale!"
"I don't want needles.
The Maraimbai is coming here today!"
"The Maraimbai is coming here?"
"It is a terrible monster.
Didn't you know men tried to get it away with guns, bazookas, and laser
    rays . . .
But it killed them all . . . and only one was left . . .
And all that he could say was 'Maraimbai . . . Maraimbai' . . ." (*horrified in
    a stupor*)
And everybody thinks he is this terrible creature.
But the peddlers had an idea.
And when we have ideas . . . it makes us safe. (*happy sigh of girl*)

So the salesman gave the girl a package full of needles.
"Put these needles around your door.
And when the Maraimbai comes
and he touches the door . . .
He will prick himself with the needles . . .
And then he will run away."

The second peddler said,
"I will give you two snakes . . .
And you put them in the water jar.
Then when the Maraimbai comes . . .
He will prick his hands on the needles . . .
He will put his hands in the water jar . . .
And he will be bitten by the snakes."
(*screams to demonstrate*)

The third salesman had a stone which weighed two hundred pounds.
He said, "Put this over your door of your bedroom.
When the Maraimbai comes . . .
He will prick his hands . . .
He will wash his hands . . .
The snakes will bite him . . .
He will run around . . .
The stone will (*sound of stone falling and crashing*)
. . . will smash him into the floor."

So the girl put the needles by the door . . .
"He will prick his hands . . ."
She put the snakes in the water jar . . .
"He will be bitten by the snakes . . ."
She put the stone over the door.
"Now the stone will fall on his head . . .
I think this will *do* it. Oh yes."
And she went under the bed.
Then she found a broomstick.
And she took that broomstick with her.

Then she heard the clock strike.
(*crying, scared sounds from girl*)
"Whoooooo . . ." (*wind sound*)

And she heard . . .
(*clomping sounds*)
(*snuffling for food sounds*)
"How do you *dare!*
There is no candy here!

I am coming into your house *now!*"

And he went to the door.
She heard him at that door . . . (*sound of squeaking door*)
(*ROAR of wounded beast*)
"Who put needles on this door!
I'll wash my hands and go to your bedroom."

He went to wash his hands and . . .
(*ROAR of wounded beast*)
"Snakes in your water jar!
I am coming to your bedroom!"

And when he came to the bedroom . . . (*sound of squeaking door . . . sound
of falling stone . . . crash*)
The two-hundred-pound stone fell . . .
And he fell flat. (*sound effect*)

And lying on the floor with that open mouth with all of those 362
teeth . . .
She did something that any normal kid would do . . .
(*WAAHHHH! WAAAHHH! WAAAHH!*)
(*girl is crying in terror . . . then slowly begins to make joyful sounds as she
sees he is stretched out*)
She went with the broomstick in her hand . . .
And she poked him. (*she makes little joyful sounds*)
And the animal didn't move.

And have you seen how when a hunter gets an animal and he puts his
foot onto the animal? She tried to do the same thing.

And she put her foot over his chest.
She began to *jump* over his chest.
But when she put her foot to give the final blow . . .

His throat was moving. (*heavy breathing*)
And a smoke started rising . . .
"I thought the thing was dead . . ."
"Yaaaahh!" It reached out and *grabbed* her!

It was going to start eating her!
And she was waving the broomstick all over.

And what would you do if an animal tried to bite your leg and you had a
broomstick in *your* hand? (*sounds of monster howling as she whacks him*)
Just like a ninja samurai!
She hit the animal for about ten minutes.

"I had no idea that a little girl like you could hit somebody with a broom-
stick so hard!"
He jumped through the window. (*OOOWWW!*)
He went away. (*girl breathing hard*)
The girl finally opened her eyes.
"He went away."
He had been gone for about two hours.
And when she looked at the floor.
There were thousands of golden stones.
They had fallen from the coat of the Maraimbai.
Because the Maraimbai liked to sleep in a bed of golden nuggets.

She went running to the store.
And she hired three hundred builders.
And she ordered them to build her the first castle with seven towers.
And instead of buying *one* bike . . .
she got herself *four* bikes. A black, a white, a purple, and a yellow one.

And one day she was riding her four bikes . . .
Guess who was there . . .
It was the Maraimbai with the three salesmen.
The man who sold the needles said:
"See I told you . . . you just have to put the needles around the door . . ."
The second one said,
"No . . . no . . . it was the snakes . . ."
The third said,
"No . . . no . . . it was the stone . . ."

She said that SHE had an effect with the broomstick!

Some people believe this is a false story.

But if you believe it is false . . . I will give you something to show that it is true.

When you go back home . . .
And it is midnight . . .

You may get yourself a nice broomstick. (*wind sounds*)
No more anything!

CABRA CABREZ

I am going to tell a *terrible* tale.[5]
The story of Cabra Cabrez.
Before I start, I want to ask you a question.
Who do you think is wiser . . . a mosquito or a dog? (*Audience guesses "dog"*)
No . . . no . . . no . . .
The mosquito.

And I am going to tell you a tale which explains *why* the mosquito is wiser than the dog.
It's the story of a rabbit.
The story of a rabbit just like you.

One morning the rabbit woke up . . . (*Roberto Carlos stretches and carries on*)
"Ahheee . . ." (*The rabbit has a little happy sigh that he gives repeatedly throughout the story*)
"I feel *sleepy!*" (*Roberto Carlos mimes some more waking up*)
He was so *cute.*
He brushed his teeth.
"Ahheee . . ."
He was so *cute.*
He combed his hair.
"Ahheee . . ."
He was so *cute.*
And every day he would find himself a big carrot.

And when he got home . . .
He would cook the carrot.

Put it in the stove.
And make himself carrot soup!
And he would drink it with a straw . . . "sluuurrrp . . . slurrrp . . ."
"Ahhheee . . ."
Ohhhh, he was really cute.

But there was a day when he went out to pick up the carrot . . .
When he went back he saw that there was a monster inside his own
    house!

He saw the eyes!
And the nose!
"Hey get away from my house! The rabbit lives here!"

"I won't leave your house!
Who is here is Cabra Cabrez!
You'd better go away or I'll split you in half!"

"Ayyyyyyy" (*squealing and fleeing*)
And the rabbit went away.
"What should I do, I have to go back to my house.
I have to get the dog.
The dog is strong.
Everybody is afraid of the dog.
Dog, come here please.
And help me take this creature away from my house."
And the dog said,
"Wooo Wooo Wooo Wooo! (*barking*)
Let me *do* it!
You know I am *very* strong.
I'll go to your house . . .
I'll get my *super* bark . . . WOOO WOOO WOOO WOOO!
And the animal will go away.
When he comes by me . . .
I will bite his back!"
"CHOMP!" "YIIII!" (*Roberto Carlos makes sounds of dog biting and ani-
    mal yelping*)

And there was the dog.

"WOO . . . nnn . . . nnn . . . WOO . . . nnn . . . WOO . . . nnn . . . nnn . . ."
(*Roberto Carlos makes sound of dog woofing and grunting along as it approaches house*)
"One . . . two . . . three . . .
"WAOO WAOO WAOO WAOO WAOO!" (*ferocious barking*)
After some time . . .

"Waoo waoo waoo all you want Mr. Dog.
Cabra Cabrez is HERE!
You'd better go away or I'll split you in half!"

"Yiiii Yiii Yiii Yiii Yiiiiiii" (*dog flees*)
And the dog went away.

The rabbit was upset.
"What can I do? The dog is afraid.
I've got an idea.
I'll call Mr. Cat.
He's really smart."

"Mr. Cat! Mr. Cat! Will you come here please?
Take this animal away from my house.
And I'll give you a bit of carrot soup."
And Mr. Cat said, "Miaouw! Miaouw!"
"Please let me do it.
I will give you my *super*'Miaouw! Miaouw!'
I am so smart.
And then it will go away."
And then he stretched . . . "Aiouwooo . . ."
And there he went.
"Miaouw . . . Miaouw . . . Miaouw . . . Miaouw . . ." (*cat is walking up in same rhythm dog used*)
"One . . . two . . . three . . . MIAOUW! MIAOUW! MIAOUW!"

After some time . . .
"Stop this Miaouw Miaouw stuff Mr. Cat.
I am Cabra Cabrez
And if you don't go away, I will split you in half!"

"Yaooowwww!"

And the cat ran away.

And the rabbit had another idea.
He could call Mr. Bull.
Mr. Bull was very big.
Everybody was afraid of Mr. Bull.
"Please Mr. Bull,
will you take this animal away from my house?
I will give you some carrot soup."

"Mmmmmooooowww . . .
I'll do it, Mr. Rabbit.
You know that Mr. Bull here is *very* strong.
I will give my super moo . . . 'Mmmmooowww . . .'
And the animal will go away.
When he comes by I will hit him
and he will never come back.
Huh . . MMM . . . mmm . . . Huh . . . MMM mmm Huh . . . MMM mmm
   Huh . . . MMM."
(*sound of bull stomping up, same rhythm as dog and cat*)

When he got to the rabbit's house, he got ready to moo . . .
"One . . . two . . . three . . . "MMMMOOOOWWWW!"

"Stop this Moo Moo thing!
I am Cabra Cabrez.
You'd better go away or I'll break you in half!"

"YOUWW!" (*sound of bull moaning as it flees*)
The bull was afraid.

And there came the mosquito.
"nnnnn . . . nnnn . . . nnnn . . . nnnn . . ."
And he landed on his nose. (*rabbit's nose*)
"nnnn . . . nnnnnn . . . n."

"Go away mosquito! Go away!"
And the mosquito went away.

But after a while . . . "nnn . . . nnnn . . . nnn . . . nnnn

I can help you."

"You are too small.
You cannot do it.
The dog couldn't do it.
The cat couldn't do it.
The bull couldn't do it.
You are too small and won't be able to help me."

"Well I am going to show you that size has nothing to do with it."
And the mosquito flew to rabbit's house.
"nnnn . . . nnnn . . . nnnn . . . nnnn . . ."
When he got there he saw Cabra Cabrez.
With his scary face.
His scary face was something like this . . . (*demonstrates*)
But the mosquito wasn't afraid of him.
He flew to the ear of Cabra Cabrez
and he went inside and made that noise that only mosquitoes and small
  kids are able to make.
"brrrrrrrrrrrrrrrrrrrrrrrrrrrrrrrr" (*high-pitched squeal*)
It was such a terrible noise.

Cabra Cabrez woke up . . . opened his eyes
and started to hit (*slapping, buzzing, slapping, buzzing*)
but the mosquito wouldn't stop.
(*slap . . . buzz . . . slap . . . buzz*)
It was so bad that Cabra Cabrez was running away from the house.
At last Cabra Cabrez was out of the house.

So Rabbit came back.
He made his soup.
And when it was ready . . .
The dog came . . .
"WOO . . . nnn . . . nnn . . . WOO . . . nnn . . . nnn . . . WOO . . . nnn . . .
  nnn . . ." (*Roberto Carlos makes sound of dog woofing and grunting along
  as it approaches house*)
"SLUUURRP." And he took a drink.
And the cat came . . .
"Miaouw . . . nnn . . . Miaouw . . . nnn . . . Miaouw . . . nnn . . . Miaouw . . ."
(*cat is walking up in same rhythm dog used*)

"SLUUURRP." And he took a drink.

And the bull came . . .

"Huh . . . MMM . . . mmm . . . Huh . . . MMM mmm Huh . . . MMM mmm Huh . . . MMM."

(*sound of bull stomping up, same rhythm as dog and cat*)

"SLUUURRP!" And he took a big drink.

But the best part of the carrot soup . . .

Can you guess who took it?

The mosquito!

And that's why I tell you this sort of thing.

It doesn't matter how small a mosquito can be, or a child.

Notes

1. Belo Horizonte Para Você, http://www.belohorizonte.mg.gov.br/por/index.php.

2. *Belo Horizonte Brazil*, pamphlet, Belo Horizonte Tourism Authority.

3. Roberto Carlos was interviewed during a visit to the MacDonald family summer home on Guemes Island during July 1999. Livia de Almeida aptly translated Robert Carlos's words. Jennifer and Nat Whitman, also tellers, provided a rapt audience. Two tapes in possession of author.

4. Transcribed from tape of Roberto Carlos telling to children at Bothell Regional Library, July 1000. Tape in possession of author. Compare this text to his written version of this story in *When the Night Is Dark in Brazil: Two Scary Tales* (1999).

5. Transcribed from tape of Roberto Carlos telling at Bothell Regional Library, July 1999. Audience of children and their parents. Telling in Portuguese, translation by Livia de Almeida. Three years later a father argued with me that Roberto Carlos *had* been telling in English. Such was his memory of the event.

Bibliography

By Roberto Carlos Ramos

Ramos, Roberto Carlos. *Marambaia*. Illus. Rosa Schettino. Belo Horizonte: Editora Dimensao, n.d.

———. *O Contador do Histórias: Roberto Carlos Ramos; O Embaixador Do País Das Maravilhas*. CD (book and cassette). © Roberto Carlos Ramos. São Paulo: FuturArte Editora Ltda, n.d.

———. *When the Night Is Dark in Brazil: Two Scary Tales*. Trans. by Livia de Almedia. Limited edition. © Roberto Carlos Ramos, 1999.

About Belo Horizonte

Eakin, Marshall C. *Tropical Capitalisim: The Industrialization of Belo Horizonte, Brazil.* New York: Palgrave, 2002.

Niemeyer, Oscar. *Pampulha.* Introduction by Juscelina Kubitschek de Oliveira. Preface by Philip Goodwin. Rio de Janeiro: Imprensa Nacional, 1944.

About Brazilian Folklore

Cascudo, Luís da Câmara. *Dictionário do Folclore.* Brasileiro São Paulo: Edições Melhoramentos, 1979.

Phra Inta Kaweewong. Photo courtesy of Margaret MacDonald.

4

Phra Inta Kaweewong

Preserving Stories in the Wat

I will use these old folktales in my sermons to the people.
Phra Inta Kaweewong

Background Information about Isaan

From 1353 to 1778, Isaan (northeastern Thailand) was a part of the Lao Kingdom. The Lao Kingdom extended on both sides of the Mekong River. But in 1778, after a war between the kingdoms, the Siamese Kingdom took over this area. The people of Isaan are culturally Lao, and until recently most spoke the Lao dialect. Exceptions are various smaller ethnic groups and the Khmer adjacent to the Cambodian border. However, the Thai government has required all schooling to be in Thai. And today the Thai mass media—TV, films, newspapers, magazines, books—have resulted in a loss of Lao-speaking skills, especially among the young.

The Isaan area is comprised of the Khorat Plateau bounded by some low mountain ranges. The Mekong River bounds the northern and western sides of the area. Our teller, Phra Inta Kaweewong, lives in Roi Et Province near the center of the plateau. Thus, his vistas are of flat rice fields extending into every distance, sprinkled by occasional lone trees. Though Isaan is physically within the boundaries of Thailand and is considered part of northeastern Thailand, Isaan refers to the area as a cultural entity, primarily Lao.

In this area the *ban,* or village, is the basic unit of Isaan life. Though each province has a larger town or small city, connections to the ban are still strong. Each ban has a *wat,* a Buddhist temple. The people grow rice, seek fish from ponds and rivers, and find certain essentials in the infrequent forested areas. The Isaan people are devout Buddhists, retaining fervent animistic beliefs at the same time.

The Monk in Isaan

Before we embark on our examination of the teller-monk, Phra Inta Kaweewong, it might be useful to speak a bit about the place of the monk in Thai life and the regular use of story made by preaching monks. The term "Phra," by the way, is an honorific title used when referring to monks. The term "wat" refers to the Thai Buddhist temple and its grounds, which can include a library, quarters for monks or nuns, and buildings for worship and study.

Prasong Saihong, raised in Ban Dong Nguu Luem, a small village in Sisaket Province, has discussed the Isaan monk at length in his master's thesis, "Storytellers in Northeast Thailand" (University of Northern Illinois, 2003).

Prasong had earlier assisted in the interview with Pra Inta Kaweewong on which this chapter is based. For his master's thesis, Prasong interviewed several other monks, along with lay storytellers, in the Mahasarakham and Roi Et provinces. In his thesis, Prasong discusses the monkhood:

In Northeast Thailand, people pay respect to Buddhism. Therefore, each person's duty is to support and preserve Buddhism. One way to support Buddhism in Northeast Thailand is for each man to serve as a monk in order to learn the *Dhamma* or Buddhist morality, or as villagers said, "the word of the Buddha," to spread that *Dhamma* to their communities. The other perspective is that by becoming a monk, each man in Northeast Thailand, reaches the stage of adulthood or "ripeness." It is believed that a man can get married only after he has passed the yellow robe. Therefore, almost every man in Northeast Thailand has to become a temporary monk. However, some men will choose to become permanent monks to study to a higher level and thereby improve their standing in society.

Due to the problem of poverty in Northeast Thailand, many men have become permanent monks. Becoming a monk is one way to get higher education. There is a school for monks or novices in each province. It is an alternative way for the male population in Northeast Thailand to get out of poverty and to get higher education. In their education, in the past monks had to learn how to read Pali or the *Dhamma* texts, and then recite, and finally take exams. However, an interview with the monks at Wat Uthaithit revealed that they studied mostly according to the Thai governmental curriculum. They did not have a chance to study the *Dhamma* script used for recording stories and documents in the past.[1]

In other words, they could not read the palm leaf manuscripts preserved in their wats.

Prasong tells us that monks use many styles of storytelling. "The first style is in prose. Second is a narration in verse known as "*Tong Toey.*" The third style is a singing style, which is unique in this area. The singing styles will be brought out on the special occasions, for example, during the *Vessantara* chant ceremony in the fourth lunar month (March), other Buddhist holy days, and so on. The singing style includes the reading of palm leaf manuscripts, which are recorded in modern Thai script, and reciting verses that the monks composed for certain kinds of ceremonies."[2]

Stories used by monks include Jataka tales (stories of the previous lives of the Buddha), *Lam Prawetsandon* or *Vesantara* chant (dealing with the last life of the Buddha), and local tales that are adaptable for teaching Buddhist principles.

Prasong interviewed two monks from Wat Utthaithit in the suburbs of the city of Mahasarkham, thus in a suburban rather than village atmosphere:

> The monks from Uthai Thit temple explained to me how they used stories in teaching and chanting nowadays. They explained that since the people could more easily understand the Buddha's principles through stories, they usually used the Buddhist moral stories in their chanting. They also chant in verse called Isan verse. They said they learned these when they studied the Buddhist Scriptures for monks. When they had spare time, they had to practice telling the stories. People may also request certain stories. When people invited them to a ceremony, they like to hear stories in "*Thet Siang*" verse and "*Lae*" verse. Thet Siang is a style of chant of moral stories with several monks taking the roles of characters in the story. *Lae* is a unique tune utilized in chanting of stories.
>
> Since the two monks stay in a big temple, they have many chances to give "*Teed nitam*" or storytelling sermons. They give sermons to lay people on the holy days, every first and the middle of Lunar calendar (every eight days). The occasion is called "*Wan Phra.*" On that day, people will offer food to monks in order to make merit. At the gathering, the lay people like to ask for stories, and then the monks tell them stories. Another important activity at *Wan Phra* is the meditation gatherings. The monks said that during med-

itation was a good time for storytelling. They told many stories that explained Buddhist principles.[3]

Prasong also interviewed Phra Inta Kaweewong, our storyteller. He compares Phra Inta's life with that of the city monks:

> Unlike the urban monks, Phra Inta has a humble and modest life in a small temple in the village of Sa-atsomboon, Roi Et. He is the abbot at the temple of the village. There will be one or two monks staying in the temple every year, some temporary monks from the village. However, he has to stay alone the rest of the year. . . . He has normal activity as other monks, which include: 1) chanting (*Tham wat*) at 4 a.m., 2) walking for food offering, 3) having lunch, and last chanting at 6 p.m. These kinds of activity seem to be boring for us, but to be a Buddhist monk, these activities will make one selfless.[4]

With this background, let us now meet our monk, Phra Inta Kaweewong.

Meet Phra Inta Kaweewong

Phra Inta was ordained as a novice when he completed the fourth grade. He was born on September 13, 1925, in Ban Kud-kwang, Tambon Muang Kao, Amphoe Muang, Changwat Khonkaen. Ban Kud-kwang is a village in Khon Kaen Province in the region of Thailand known as Isaan. Since the region is culturally a part of Thailand but the major culture in Isaan is Lao, Phra Inta would speak both Thai and Lao. It is quite usual for young boys in this area to become novitiates at a young age. They may enter the monastery for a short period of time, or they may be raised by the monks.

At the age of twenty, Phra Inta was ordained as a monk. Around 1948, while still in the monkhood, Phra Inta began to compose Isaan poetry, working in *klon lam,* poetry for singing *lam,* Isaan folk tunes, *kham klon,* other Isaan poetic forms, and *lae uay phon,* a type of Isaan verse written and sung for giving blessings and used on special occasions, when requesting donations, and when telling certain stories.

Phra Inta wrote under the pen name of "O. Kaweewong." The "O" is pronounced like the "o" in "or" without the "r" sound.

In 1951 Phra Inta left the monkhood and began working at Khlang Nana Witthaya Printing House. While there, he wrote *klon* for *mo lam muu* (Isaan folk operas with traditional costumes), verse tales for individual Isaan folk singers, and *lam phoen* (Isaan folk operas with modern costumes and jazzy music). His verses were used by many Isaan folk opera groups and were quite popular in those days.

During the time that Phra Inta was in the monkhood, he also learned to read palm leaf manuscripts. This is a skill that not many people, even monks, can accomplish today. Many ancient stories are written on these palm leaf texts and are stored in the various wats throughout the country. Few monks can read them today, and they are gradually being lost to mildew, vermin, and neglect. Phra Inta has rescued some of these texts by transcribing them and arranging for their publication in book form.

Phra Inta reentered the monkhood and today resides at Wat Sa-ahd-somboon, Tamboon Sa-ahdsomboon, Amphoe Muang, Changwat Roi Et. He uses stories in his sermons and, at the urging of Dr. Wajuppa Tossa, he recently began writing his stories down in notebooks. Phra Inta writes the tales down as he remembers them on notebooks provided by Dr. Wajuppa. Then he returns them to her, and Prasong Saihong enters the tales into a database and uses them as source material to instruct university students in storytelling. Thus, the stories are being revived and restored as a living art form.

About the Interview

I first meet Phra Inta when Dr. Wajuppa invited him to speak at our 1996 Tellabration ceremonies at Mahasarakham University. Tellabration is a worldwide storytelling event sponsored by the National Storytelling Network in Jonesborough, Tennessee. I was teaching with Dr. Wajuppa that quarter as a Fulbright Scholar. We were training university students in storytelling arts and were beginning to tour with them to school districts throughout Isaan. Dr. Wajuppa seized upon the notion of a worldwide storytelling day, Tellabration, as an opportunity to excite teachers in her area about the joys of storytelling. In addition to the storytelling performances throughout the weekend, she arranged for Phra Inta, two traditional *mo lam* singers, and a *khaen* player to discuss folklore traditions in a panel. He graciously returned to speak for us at our Tellabrations the two following years as well.

Later I was fortunate to visit Phra Inta at the wat to hear him read aloud from a palm leaf manuscript text that he had transcribed for publication. Dr. Wajuppa had been working on an English-language translation of this text and wanted to hear him interpret it orally. We arrived unannounced on a hot afternoon, and Phra Inta was napping. But he graciously came to make us welcome and respond to our needs. After we had waited and settled ourselves discreetly, Phra Inta took out his text and began to read. He sat erect and read in round tones, without faltering, for more than an hour and a half. A lone fly buzzed around the golden Buddha statues at the side of the hall, and a child, left for babysitting with an elderly monk, toddled about the courtyard behind us. Other than that, nothing moved in the wat that still afternoon as Phra Inta intoned the precious text.

The next time I was fortunate to hear Phra Inta, we were holding a story-telling retreat for teachers at Nadoon, a folk museum in Mahasarakham Province. Again it was a hot afternoon. But this time about fifty teachers were crowded into a conference center on classroom chairs, clustering to hear Phra Inta, who sat on a wooden chair in front of them. The usual formality of the monkhood seemed missing from this event, and Phra Inta told folktales in a lively fashion. Then, spurred on by encouragement from his appreciative audience, he told even more.

Later that year (May 22, 1997), Dr. Wajuppa returned to interview Phra Inta with questions I had sent for this book, coupled with some queries of her own. Prasong Saihong accompanied her and later translated Phra Inta's stories from Lao into English. Prasong was later to become a student of Phra Inta and do a ten-day novitiate at the wat. In the interviews, Phra Inta is addressed respectfully as Luang Phaw.

The Interview

Phra Inta was asked how he had learned stories.

Stories were read from palm leaf manuscripts in order to give sermons to the folks who come to listen. Later, those folks would remember the stories and retell them in the rice fields and farms. And at night, when someone died, they retold those stories to each other. That was the origin of telling stories in the old times.

Luang Phaw, have you known anyone in your village who used to tell stories? In the village where you grew up?

At that time, when I was young, there was an old man named Phaw Nuan Labunthian. He was a storyteller. He liked to tell stories to people when people sat together talking, when there was a village meeting. He told stories to others. I remembered Phaw Nuan stories and ideas and retold those stories. It was the ideas of the old-time folks.

Your career of composing stories and telling stories, when did that begin?

Seriously, it began in the year 1947. I began to compose stories. In Isaan in those days, people liked to listen to stories. People were interested in listening to old folktales. The market, the printers, wanted to publish and distribute the folktales. So they published all these folktales. They ordered the people who could write and compose tales, who could compose tales in verse, to give them those tales, and they published them.

In the old times, on what occasions did they tell stories?

They took the occasions to tell stories when there were social gatherings. Funeral wakes, someone dies, making merit, celebrations. During free time, people came to sit and talk under trees and stilt houses . . . in the house compound. People liked to listen to stories. They did not want to hear other things.

People did not have jobs like today. They had nothing to do; they told stories when they did not have jobs to do. They entertained themselves by telling and listening to stories when they did not go to work [when the rice-planting season was over].

For funeral wakes, besides telling stories, they read stories from palm leaf manuscripts too, correct?

Besides telling stories in funeral wakes, people liked to listen to stories being read from palm leaf manuscripts too. They read in various tunes. So people were interested. They were moved by the tunes and stories. They could feel sad. They could laugh. And they enjoyed the stories together.

In terms of stories, people liked that. Besides telling stories and reading palm leaf manuscripts for entertainment, people in those days had nothing. Because there were no dramas, plays, or operas. Nothing besides stories. Stories released people from tension and grief.

When young men in the past courted or wooed women, they told stories. Is that true?

Sometimes after finishing work at the rice field, young men would go to woo or court women, talk to women. After eating rice and fish (dinner), young men would go to woo young women at that and this house. Young women were engaging in activities such as separating cocoons, spinning thread (silk and cotton). When young men visited young women, they liked to tell stories sometimes for pleasure and enjoyment.

What are some of the stories that you used to tell?

I used to tell the stories of Thao Suriwong (Prince Suriwong), Khulu Nang Ua, Phadaeng Nang Ai, The Blind Touched the Elephant, The Blind

Man, and the Man with Glued Legs. These latter two tales were funny, and children liked them a lot. Kaew Na Ma (The Horse-Face Girl). I used to tell that too.

In those days I told in everyday spoken language mixed with verse alternately. It's called "Stories in *Tong Toey*." If I told in only spoken words, it was no fun. Just like the way I retold a story at the university (during Tellabration 1996). In the old times, people did not like to speak plain everyday language. They liked to speak and mix poetry in their speeches. This was called *Tong Toey* and *Phaya* (proverbs in verse). So telling stories promoted and helped to maintain *Phaya* and *Tong Toey*.

How do you use stories nowadays?

I mostly tell tales to old people who visit the temple, once in a long while. Tales from the *Phra Traipidok* (Tripitaka, Buddhist Scriptures). Like *Phra Chao Ha Roi Chaht* (Tales of the five hundred past lives of the Buddha). Or *Phra Dhammabot* (the tales from the Buddha's *Dhamma,* teachings). Old tales are told once in a long while.

What is the significance of local folktales?

Local folktales have morals to remind people to think of ancestors from the old times. To think of their ways of life, their wisdom, and their stupidity. People in the modern times can listen and compare themselves with those in the old times. The listeners now, if they have intelligence and wisdom, they can gain morals, pleasure, and enjoyment when listening.

From Luang Phaw's observations, what stories do children and old people like to hear now?

From my observations, children, younger, and young people like to listen to comic stories, jokes, and funny stories. Anything to make them laugh with pleasure. Even old people like those funny stories too. The funnier the stories, the more they enjoy listening.

Luang Phaw, according to your ideas, what can be done to revive the folktales?

I think we can revive the local folktales. We must bring the old tales to use in sermons.

And use them to give illustrations to the people who come to listen to sermons and the Buddha's *Dhamma*. These old people, after hearing the old stories, will recall the old stories. And that will revive the old folktales. The old people will retell the stories to their children and their grandchildren.

These young people will be interested in old folktales. During Buddhist Lent, I will use these old folktales in my sermons to the people.

Is it true that the printer has come to contact Luang Phaw to recollect these old tales?

Some stories, those without the original manuscripts, they want. Some stories have been lost. When they lost the original manuscripts, they asked me to rewrite. For example they asked me to rewrite the stories of *Suriyakhrat* (Eclipse), *Chathakhrat* (Lunar Eclipse), or the story of the frog eating the sun and the moon.

Where were the original manuscripts of the Isaan folktales from?

The original manuscripts are from palm leaf manuscripts in wats. The storytellers and composers are unknown. Nobody was interested to know. I assume they were ancient poets and storytellers before I was born. If you want to know the name, you have to look at the palm leaf manuscripts. There may be a day, month, and year it was recorded.

Thank you, Luang Phaw, for taking your time to answer these questions. Now would you want to tell us a story?

Phra Inta's Stories

THE THREE FRIENDS

Once, long ago,
there were three animals,
a quail, a monkey, and an elephant.
They lived in a banyan tree in the Himmavanta Forest.
In the morning, each would go to find food according to its nature.
In the evening, each would always come to sleep at the tree.

One day, the three animals happened to meet and talk.
The quail said, "Three of us have lived here for a long time.
But never have we had a chance to talk to each other.
Today we have a good opportunity.
Why don't we become friends and get to know and understand each
    other?

Then we shall respect each other.
I would like to know who was born first.
Whoever was born first should be elected as our well-revered and well-
respected leader."

The elephant said, "When I was born, my mother brought me here to
find food.
I saw this banyan tree. It was about the height of my stomach.
I walked over it every day."
The monkey said, "The elephant must be born after me.
When I was born, my mother brought me here.
I saw the banyan tree. It was as tall as my head."

The quail said, "When I was born,
I flew to eat berries at a tree that grew way over there.
I flew to excrete here.
This banyan tree grew because of my droppings.
So, I was born before you, my two friends."

From then on, the elephant and the monkey accepted the quail as their
leader.
They gave full respect to him as their elder brother, who was older than
they were.
The quail also behaved respectably.
He was well respected by his friends since that time.

In sum, whether one is a human being or an animal,
one's life will be forever filled with happiness, success, and contentment,
if one is respectful to others.

Those inferior and superior, those older and more knowledgeable than
oneself,
and those who are less knowledgeable.
In addition, one must not be stubborn or pigheaded.

THE KING WHO MAKES DREAMS COME TRUE

King Phrommathat of Pharanasi was once known for his greatness.
His kingdom became the most prosperous and his people the most
contented.

The king could give his people everything.

"Did I give my people everything?" wondered King Phrommathat.

"Yes, everything . . . except for . . . their dreams," he thought.

"But as I am the greatest king, I should be able to give them everything, even their dreams."

So, the next day, the king made a proclamation to his people.

"From now on, tell me your dream. I will make everyone's dream come true."

The people of Pharanasi then went to have audience with their king daily, to recount their dreams from the previous night whereby the king fulfilled their every dream.

One day, an old man walked into the palace to have an audience with the king.

"Your Highness, last night I dreamed that I was married to the daughter of the richest man in the kingdom."

"Your dream will come true tomorrow," promised the king,

"I will order the rich man to have an audience with me first."

The old man was so overwhelmed with joy.

"I will be the happiest man on earth. The rich man's daughter is so young and beautiful."

He was so overjoyed that he could not help himself.

On his way home, he walked by the rich man's house to see the rich man's daughter. Once there, he said to the rich man,

"I dreamed that I married your daughter last night and I have informed the king about it. He will arrange the wedding for me tomorrow."

The rich man was alarmed but he called his daughter to let her know about it.

The rich man's daughter was a very smart girl.

She said to the old man,

"Oh, dear Grandfather, if the king orders us, we must follow his command.

But we must wait for his order.

Today, you must return to wait at your house first.

When I receive the order from the king, I will be your wife."

The old man returned home happily.

He could hardly wait to have such a young and beautiful girl for his wife.

The rich man asked his daughter, "Do you think you can really follow the king's command, my daughter?"

"Oh, no, Father, the old man is old enough to be my grandfather.

I cannot marry him, but we have to think of how to get out of this situation," she answered.

They continued discussing the matter until late that night.

Finally, the girl came up with a brilliant plan.

They asked their gardener to help to execute the plan.

Early the next morning, the rich man's gardener went to have an audience with the king. He was the first one on that day. So, he asked,

"Your Majesty, is it true, as I was told, that you would grant your people their dreams?"

"Yes, what is your dream?" the king asked.

"Then, I am the happiest man on earth."

The gardener continued, "I dreamed that I married the queen last night."

The king was infuriated,

"How dare you dream that you married my wife!"

"I am not giving you my wife. This is not right.

You are just a gardener; how can you marry a queen?

Now off with your arrogant head."

Before the guards arrived, the gardener said,

"Please have mercy on me.

You already gave me your word that you would give me my dream.

I am following your command.

You cannot talk about right or wrong now.

Even the old man who was old enough to be the girl's grandfather was allowed to be married to a young woman of fourteen."

The king was speechless.

After awhile, he said, "All right, then, I will stop this command from now on.

You are not going to marry my wife.

The old man is not going to marry the rich man's daughter."

So ended the vain command of King Phrommathat of Pharanasi.

And so ends the tale of "The King Who Makes Dreams Come True."

Notes

1. Prasong Saihong, "Storytelling in Northeast Thailand," Master's thesis, University of Northern Illinois, 2003, p. 17.
2. Ibid., 56.
3. Ibid., 57.
4. Ibid., 58.

Bibliography

Sources to Learn More about Thai Buddhism and Culture

Saihong, Prasong. "Storytelling in Northeast Thailand." Master's thesis, University of Northern Illinois, 2003.

Tambiah, S. J. *Buddhism and the Spirit Cults in North-East Thailand.* Cambridge: University Press, 1970. Detailed discussion of the Thai Buddhist monk. Also discusses the training and work of the *paahm* (derived from the Hindu word *brahamn*). This spirit leader emerges from the Hindu ancestry and is an important Thai religious figure. Often the *paahm* is a leader in the Buddhist community, usually a former monk or novice.

Tossa, Wajuppa. "Isaan Storytelling." In *Festival of American Folklife,* 52. Washington, D.C.: Smithsonian Institution, 1974. Discusses ritual storytelling of Thai Buddhist monks in Isaan.

———. *Padang Nang Aie: A Translation of a Thai Folk-Epic in Verse.* Lewisburg: Bucknell University Press; London: Associated University Presses, 1990.

———. *Phya Khankhaak, the Toad King: A Translation of an Isan Fertility Myth in Verse.* Trans. Wajuppa Tossa. Original transcription by Phra Ariyanuwat. Lewisburg: Bucknell University Press; London: Associated University Presses, 1996. Translation of Isan epic preserved as palm leaf manuscript in temple.

Vathanaprida, Supaporn. *Thai Tales: Folktales from Thailand.* Englewood, Colo.: Libraries Unlimited, 1994.

Makia Malo. Photo courtesy of Margaret MacDonald.

5

Makia Malo

Standing in Front of Them

*They read the message . . . the other message . . . that it's not
the stories I'm telling. It's the fact that I'm standing in front
of them. Sharing the stories.*
    MAKIA MALO

BACKGROUND INFORMATION ABOUT HANSEN'S DISEASE, KALAUPAPA, AND HAWAIIAN HOMESTEAD LANDS

Hansen's Disease

Our teller was diagnosed with Hansen's disease at the age of twelve and exiled to Kalaupapa. People with this disease prefer this term to the term "leprosy" with its many bad connotations. In particular, the term "leper" is offensive. The disease is caused by a germ, mycobacterium leprae, and affects the nerves, skin, and eyes. Since the mid-1940s, sulfone drugs have been used to treat this disease. Individuals who take their medication regularly halt the disease; the disease no longer progresses, and they are no longer contagious to others.[1]

Kalaupapa

In January 1866 a group of patients (9 men and 2 women) were dropped off on the southeastern side of the Kalaupapa Peninsula. They were expected to fend for themselves, but this proved untenable for the sick patients. By October, the number of patients had risen to 142 as more were dropped off. The Board of Health made some efforts to improve things, but it was with the arrival of Father Damien in 1873 that the settlement came into caring and competent hands. Father Damien died of leprosy in 1889, but his service to the colony is legendary. The twentieth century saw increased improvements in the life of the community. When former governor Lawrence Judd arrived in 1947 as superintendent, many of the more onerous facts of the community's life fell away. New medicine could halt the progress of the disease and render the patients noncontagious. So, rules about contact with outsiders were lifted. In 1967, the outdated laws governing patients were abolished. Today, Hansen's disease patients are free to leave Kalaupapa and live wherever they choose. Several older residents, however, have chosen to stay in the place they call home. This peninsula is in fact one of the most beautiful spots on earth. Surrounded by blue seas and backed by towering green pali, or cliffs, it is truly a tropical paradise—now. Once the residents no longer need this preserve, the area will become a national park. It is now under park auspices.[2]

Hawaiian Homestead Lands

Under pressure from Prince Kuhio of Hawaii and his supporters, the U.S. Congress passed the Hawaiian Homestead Act of 1920. Approximately 290,000 acres are placed in trust for the Hawaiian people. Up to this day, Hawaiians of at least 50 percent Hawaiian blood can apply for homestead land, though the assets no longer meet the needs. The settled land forms Hawaiian communities such as Papakolea on the slopes of Punchbowl Crater above Honolulu.[3] This was Makia's home.

Meet Makia Malo

Makia Malo spent his young childhood in the Hawaiian homestead community of Papakolea. This tight-knit Hawaiian enclave is perched high above Honolulu, on the slopes of Punchbowl Crater. Makia tells rich stories of these technicolor days of childhood—ti-leaf sliding on Punchbowl, picking guava up the valleys, and hard-working weekends in the taro patches down country at Laiea.

Makia and his kid brother, Pele, made a rascally team, wrestling together and tearing around the neighborhood. But a cloud hung over the Malo family. Leprosy had begun to ravage its way through the children. Already his older sister had been sent to Kalaupapa for treatment, leaving behind her own little girl for Makia's mother to raise. Next, when Makia was nine, his kid brother Pele was also diagnosed with Hansen's disease and removed from the family. And three years later, it was Makia's turn.

The stigma of the disease was so great in those days that once it was known that a family hosted leprosy, social contacts within the community were severed. Removal to Kalaupapa for treatment was in effect exile for life. This small, isolated peninsula on the southwestern shore of the island of Molokai was isolated from the rest of Molokai by steep palis and made an effective natural prison. The only approaches were by mule train down the steep cliff or by sea. Air service was finally begun in the summer of 1947, just months before Makia was removed to the settlement.

But to twelve-year-old Makia, Kalaupapa presented wonders as well as horrors. Removed from the urban restrictions of Honolulu, the young teen now found himself free to roam eleven acres from sea to mountain! And the loss of his mother was offset by the joy of being reunited with his "partner in crime," his kid brother Pele. Now, Makia's older sister became his surrogate mother, raising Makia at Kalaupapa while their mother raised the sister's child back at Papakoleo.

Makia tells many stories of those happy Kalaupapa teen years—pig hunting in the mountains, picnicking at the beach, singing away the night with his buddies on the pier. He tells too of the horror he felt when first getting to know the elderly patients, whose ravaged visages struck terror into the heart of a child. He expresses this childhood terror in the prose poem "Katie's Store."[4]

Makia's teen years gave way to adulthood. The disease pursued its course. By age thirty Makia had lost his sight. Now Makia raged at imprisonment. Confined to his room and a small area of the compound between his quarters and the cafeteria, Makia lost his joy in living and despaired. Then a short story he had written won a contest, and a social worker asked him what he would do if he could have a dream. Makia opened his inner eyes and *did* begin to dream. Medicine now had been developed that allowed individuals with the disease to reenter society, if they chose to do so. But this disease leaves unkind marks on its victims, and it took great courage to face the constant stares of the outside world.

In 1972, at the age of thirty-seven, Makia Malo returned to Honolulu to begin his reentry into society. His first months were a trial. But Makia endured and entered the University of Hawaii to begin pursuing that dream he had allowed himself to embrace. Makia graduated with a bachelor's degree in Hawaiian studies and went on to receive his secondary education teaching certificate.

In those days, the Honolulu Parks Department employed handicapped individuals to assist with its programs. After taking a short storytelling course with park storyteller Jeff Gere, Makia found his niche. As more and more opportunities to tell arose, Makia's skills strengthened. For a time he performed with Nona Beamer and others in artist-in-the-schools theatrical productions. When "Auntie Nona" retired, Makia was left with the job of emceeing the shows. Eventually, he realized that he could do artists-in-the-schools programs alone, as a storyteller. Now, Makia, with the help of his new wife Ann, has begun to put his stories and prose poems into print. He has also begun to tour extensively throughout the United States and to the South Pacific, Japan, and Europe.

Though Makia and Ann live in a Honolulu apartment, Makia chooses to retain a Kalaupapa cottage rather than receive a stipend to help with his living expenses in Honolulu. Only a handful of patients still reside at Kalaupapa. They are mostly elderly folks who prefer to remain at home in the place they know, secure in a spot where no one stares at their alarming facial configurations. Makia and Ann retreat to his cottage in this beautiful but increasingly lonely spot to think, write stories, and renew themselves. And for Makia, this is also a time to touch old friends and to remember.

Talking with Makia

I interviewed Makia in his Kalaupapa cottage one windy November day.[5] His guide dog, Inca Blue, lay patiently in his corner, and in the next room Ann chatted quietly with elderly neighbor Lucy. Outside the winds rushed in from the sea to whip the palms and wear themselves out against the dark palis behind the house. Makia and I sat upright at the little wooden table with the tape recorder between us, and he did what he does best—talked story.

Later, we drove in one of Kalaupapa's decrepit but dependable vehicles down to the beach at the end of Kalaupapa's road and had more talk. Talk of picnics, ball games, swimming spots, and friends. So many friends. So many good times. Despite the bad.

Sharing Kalaupapa

While he was still a student at the University of Hawaii, Makia began to be invited to speak about Kalaupapa.

It seems as if I took it on as my . . . my cross . . . my crusade . . . to talk about Kaluapapa. So that the people on the outside came to know me. And in that way hopefully make it easier for someone else to leave if they ever wanted to.

But I think the main thing I learned is . . . in doing these things . . . talking about Kalaupapa and myself, being blind and the whole thing . . . that it made things very easy for me being out in the community. I didn't have to hide anymore. I didn't have to be embarrassed.

So basically it was sharing the history of Kalaupapa. But, when I got into storytelling . . . the history itself . . . I think personally I realized the uniqueness of it. Fabulous story. But how to get it as part of my storytelling thing? It came through long and hard. It took a few years. But it did come.

Many people knew about Kaluapapa. But they didn't know what it was like, the daily things of kids like us, who grew up in this place. So I realized that the stories I share are unique in the sense that they come from a place like this. But it's a common story, because it could have happened anywhere in the world . . . not necessarily Kalaupapa.

Beginning to Tell

Makia points out that his formal training as a storyteller is limited.

For me I've come to realize what kind of storyteller I am . . . the "Talk Story" style of Hawaii. Which is just an informal gathering. And everybody does it . . . with their friends, with their family, with their mom, with their dad . . . anytime you speak you share a story. So for me it was just easy because that's how we talk here in Kalaupapa.

At times Makia would become terrified onstage. He has developed a technique for dealing with this stage fright.

I think the main ingredient for me, that made me stronger in a sense . . . was to realize that all I needed to do was talk to one friend. So whenever I am storytelling that is all I'm doing. When I first got in touch with that idea it was kind of difficult, because my mind was going every which way. Especially when I panicked. I couldn't get in touch with it. But enough times have passed where I automatically . . . go into that spot . . . when I am nervous. And all I see is this one friend . . . sharing an intimate story. So as relaxed or whatever people see me on the stage . . . I am just talking to one friend, you know. I am comfortable and confident enough to know now that there is a crowd out there. Still it's the imagery . . . there still is that one friend out there . . . that I'm sharing a story with.

The Unspoken Message

But what is most significant is the unspoken message . . .
    the unstated message . . .
    that certain kids pick up.
    We got a letter one day from one of the students.
    And she said that the counselor was after her,
    that she was graduating soon
    and so she should get some counseling in preparation to enter college.
    And she said, "I'm not going to college."
    She had no idea of going to college.
    So I went there to speak.
    And after the presentation I got this letter saying that . . .
    right after we got through she went to see her advisor and said,
    "If he can do it . . . I can too."
    It's that kind of message the kids pick up.
    I mean we don't tell them, right?
    They just pick it up on their own.

    One of the kids . . .
    I was sharing about how I felt when I first left.
    I felt so conspicuous.
    My hands . . . I used to keep them under my shirt.
    I'd walk all over town like I'm carrying a gun . . . or a bomb.
    My hands sticking in my pocket.
    I was ashamed about my hands.
    They seemed so obvious . . . disfigured . . .
    This letter was . . .
    "I know what you mean kapuna." Kapuna is elder or grandparent.
    He said,
    "I know what you mean kapuna, because I hate it when they call me
        "special ed."
    That kind of label, you know.

    Or this kid . . . a letter from this girl.
    Because I talk about leprosy.
    I talk about blindness.
    Whatever questions the kids ask me, I try to put it as straight as I can.

So this kid was saying how she knows about being embarrassed because
   she feels bad when her grandmother walks her to school and then
   people stare at the grandmother.
Well obviously the grandmother had the disease.
Showed the signs.
And the kid said that nobody wants to talk to her grandmother.
So her grandmother leaves her off at the school,
and nobody goes out and says hello to her grandmother.
And she has to go to class.

We have a lot of letters from kids saying, "Oh, they like the stories . . . the
   stories are fun . . . we love your dog . . . we love your wife too, you know."
But it's these letters . . . these special letters that come.
And they read the message . . . the other message . . .
that it's not the stories I'm telling.
It's the fact that I'm standing in front of them.
Sharing the stories.

Tradition

*Though Makia came from a family with Hawaiian literary traditions, he was
not aware of that fact. An ancestor, David Malo, was the first Hawaiian writer
of note. And Makia's own grandfather was a great chanter, but Makia did not
know about that when he was young. When I asked about storytellers he had
heard, Makia did not recall any, but then I asked about folks "talking story."*

Oh yeah! The old folks would be sitting around, you know. They'd be
sitting around at luaus . . . or family gatherings . . . or funerals. They'd be sitting down . . . and then we'd hear . . . a little bit, you know . . . not much.

Years later, I remember talking to my dad. What my dad said, and it's a
shame because I find it out late, that his father was a great chanter in his day.

And he had a very good friend whose name was Lokaii . . .
and when my grandfather died,
Lokaii lived way down at Kahuku.
And he caught the train to come all the way to Laeia.
And my dad said the depot is about two miles from the house.
And the people were all waiting for Lokaii.
As soon as the train stopped, Lokaii got off.
He was already chanting. In honor of my grandfather.

He chanted all the way from the depot up to the house.
Where my grandfather was lying in the coffin.
I never heard these stories before.
My folks never shared.
Nothing.

Story Material: Makia Turns to Books of Hawaiian Legends

But I was looking for stories to tell. I didn't have any stories so I started memorizing legends, yeah? I couldn't see me doing legends. So . . . I memorized one. You know the story about Laka and the Canoe? It's well known across the Pacific. Well, I started doing that. Dry as it comes out of the book.

But the one day . . . I remember I was in Kailua and I told myself. "You've been using that damn story so many times. Geez. You've gotta get new stories." And all of a sudden . . . out of sheer panic, I switched the whole thing into . . . *pidgin*. Kent Bowman was a classic storyteller in pidgin. [Bowman's recordings of stories retold in Hawaiian pidgin were popular in the islands.] So remembering that, that's what I did. A complete turnaround.

I talk about Laka. Laka in the story he's an eight-year-old . . . ten-year-old boy . . . goes out to cut a tree. My Laka was fifteen years old. Drop-off from high school. You know. Just cruising. Nothing to do. So he . . . the complete format I guess changed, but the story's the same. He tells his momma he's going out to the mountain to make a canoe. And his momma gets so puzzled. Because he has a hard time fixing his own bed. He leaving his room *mokakai.* You know, all upset. And he's going out to the mountain make one canoe? She can't put things together. So he goes to borrow his daddy's adze. Cause his daddy got the adze, the best that Sears Roebuck can offer from the catalogue. You know, he pick up the adze. He take 'em along. And he goin' cut down this tree. Of course, Hawaiians being respectful of nature, you gotta make a sacrifice.

Oh, before he left home his mother had to make a *bento* for him in his backpack, you know. (*I laugh, "A little Japanese in there?"*) Yeah. Everything! Everything! His mother was the best cook. She made the best *dimuguan. Dimuguan* is a Filipino dish. So. I mean *all* that kind of stuff. So late at night when he is waiting. In the evening he's with his daddy. You know, go in the back parts. Get the guitar, sing *pickalimea* to serenade themselves. Drink Kirin tea. Just to pass the time. And then nine o'clock he's going to sleep. So I ask the kids. "You know how he could tell what time? When he knew it was nine o'clock?" The kids all guess . . . say "the moon?" . . . say "the wind?" . . . they try to guess. I say, "No. He look at his Seiko watch."

So I had the kids just roaring. But that saved me . . . you know. Looking back in retrospect, I think what it started to give me was the ease . . . the comfortability I needed.

Makia received experience working with a microphone and handling large groups when he joined Nona Beamer and others in an artists-in-the-schools program.

At first Nona acted as emcee. But after a while she decided to move back to the Big Island. So that left me with the microphone! For me, I didn't put it together until that time. But all of a sudden Auntie Nona was gone and I was narrating stories. The other four would be dramatizing the story and I just *waxed heavy!* And I tell the kids. Don't play. Otherwise you gonna miss some of the story. And I just go . . . the exciting part my voice gets *louder* and I talk *faster*. Then when it gets spooky I come down so slow and I whispering to it. For me, I was having a ball. And that's when

I started to find *me* as a storyteller.

But still, I needed stories. And then I found out the stories that were on my first cassette started to take hold. And it started to become more comfortable for me. Picking around things that worked. Picking . . . and chucking the things that didn't work. Just by trial and error . . . I started to survive.

At that time Makia was still receiving five dollars an hour for his storytelling work. As his skills improved, he realized that he could now perform in schools on his own as an artist-in-the-schools and perhaps make his living doing this work that he enjoyed so much. At a gathering at the University of Hawaii, he ran into storyteller Lynn Marshall.

I paid my dues those times you know.

Five dollars an hour.

And so, I became part of the storytelling people.

We were talking about who makes what . . .

and Marshall said, "You know when they ask me for a storyteller, I tell them.

You pay me one hundred dollars. I'm worth a hundred dollars."

God, that was an eye-opener for me.

I have trouble asking even for five dollars to be paid.

And her, she is demanding one hundred dollars.

She's not asking, she's not begging.

She's telling.

I'm worth a hundred dollars dollars.

I thought that was soooo fabulous!

It was just about that time that Ann came into my life. I knew if she would work with me we could have a fabulous program together. And so finally she started to come with me. But at the beginning I have to admit . . . I didn't realize it. The material was all mine. They weren't written. They were all extemporaneous. But they were subjects that . . . I'm going to have to write that down. But then . . . I came to the point that I had to share it with Ann. That Ann has to take some of it off of me. And I started to get upset. I didn't know why at the time. But then, the basic thing was running through my mind . . . it's *my* stuff . . . it's *my* material. You know she can talk about leprosy. She can talk all of this other stuff . . . this historical stuff . . . but not the stuff I'm doing. Until I started to give away some of that stuff to her. Then we could move faster.

For several years Ann and Makia toured together. Ann offered introduction and fended questions from the audience, surrounding Makia's performance with commentary and clarification. Makia's instinct was right. Together they made a fabulous team. Unfortunately, Ann's health no longer allows this. Ann sends this request from Makia and is reprinted from his publicity packet.

I want to beg you to please refrain from using the word "leper." True, Father Damien used it and it is in the Bible, but that was such a long, long time ago. Words and feelings about words change.

Today, the word "leper" is our new battle. It embarrasses, insults, and shames us. It reduces us to what may be the most repugnant image in language. It makes us separate from you. It hurts.

Actually, there is no such thing as "a leper." There are only people. You will always be on safe ground if you "Put people first," before their disease or condition. Please say, not a leper, but a *person* who had Hansen's disease; not a cripple, but a *person* whose legs are paralyzed, etc. It is not only a kinder thing to say, it is really a more accurate thing to say. Thank you for trying. Thank you very much.

Makia's Stories

THE GUAVA MAN

Makia loves to tell stories of his youth, both growing up in Papakolea, the Hawaiian homestead lands above Punchbowl Crater in Honolulu, and in Kalaupapa. At times he shapes these memories into story-poems. Here is the way he told me "The Guava Man" that day in his Kalaupapa cottage.

The guava man came.
An empty sack over his shoulder.
He was tall, spare.
Short tufts of white hair pulled down from under his floppy hat.
That shaded a real craggy face.
A meerschaum pipe gripped firmly in his teeth.
And with a gnarled walking stick . . . he moved . . .
In a cloud of tobacco smoke.

"*Aaaayyy!* The guava man *here!*" echoed down the land.

"The guava man *here!*"
and the message spread.

And voices attached to little brown children were everywhere . . .
As Lilliputians from Gulliver.

"If we go out to pick guava, you *pay* us."

"Yes, of course. But . . . can't pay all of you. Sorry.
Don't have enough money to pay all of you.
Just need a few good workers.
Maybe four."

"Me mister! Me mister!" Hands raised, fingering the air.
Eager eyes, searching the wrinkled face.
He was familiar to us, this man.
He had been here before.
"OK! OK! You . . . you . . . you . . . and you."

Others watched, as the lucky four ran ahead of the *haole*.
To where the pungent smell of ripened guava hung heavy in the air.

For summer is high season.
The trees are low.
Fruits easy to pluck.
And I pick *plenty.*
"One for the *haole* . . .
and one for me.
One for the *haole* . . .

And one for me."
Breath sweetened with guava.
T-shirt stained and hands thrust forward,
We approach the *haole* in triumph.

I was lucky that day.
I earn fifteen cents for half an hour.
Picking guava.

THE FIRST TIME I KILLED A CHICKEN

One of Makia's favorite tales is the story of abortive attempts to kill a chicken when he was a teenager.[6] Though it is a bit gory, Makia's skillful pacing make this an intriguing story.
This story takes place in 1948
and in those year, the airport isn't the way it is now.
Before, no terminal, just road and macadam strip.
At the end of the runway was a beach house.
Owned by Bill and Nancy.
Down there for a holiday.

One day we had a visitor.
A woman came from Honolulu.

And Jimmy and I coming back from the beach.
And the lady of the house, Nancy, called out,
She said, "Makia! You know how for kill chicken?"

"How kill *chicken*?
I never kill chicken before."

"Never mind. Never mind.
You gone kill the chicken."

"Aaaaahhhh . . ."
So I looked at that guy Jimmy.
He was about seventeen at the time.
I said, "Jimmy? You know how for kill chicken?"
He tell me no.

Well I guess I never learned to like, you know, look like a *lolo*.
You know . . . kind of retarded, yeah?

So I was walking to the house kind of cool, you know.
Cause it's the first time Nancy had asked me to do something respons-
  ible.
Actually she preferred my kid brother to me.
So her asking me was little strange. But still . . .

Go to the house.
Go through the kitchen.
As we're passing through the kitchen I see this *long* kind knife . . . that
  cooks use . . . to chop vegetables.
Big handle. But the *blade* is so long on the body. Sixteen inches long. To a
  long point.
So I saw this knife on a counter.
So I grab 'em.

So Kimo and I walk out through the back door.
And there was a small porch.
And as soon as I step out . . . I saw this chicken.
Strutting in the back yard.
In front of the stone wall.
The oldest chicken I ever saw in my life.
Great rooster you know!
One real *old* rooster.
And I *looooking* at it.
Wow.
And you know how rooster's throat . . . the skin . . .

I said, "Jimmy, I go get the chicken.
I hold him.
And then you cut the throat."

"Noo. Noo."

Well. The responsibility was mine.
So I . . . *oooohhhh* I look *eeeehhhh* the chicken got *up!*
So I give him the knife.
I told him, "Here. Here. Hold that knife."

So I *ran* over there.

And I grabbed . . .

What they did was . . . the end of the line . . . they nailed it into the
ground.

So I got that line. I pulled that nail out.

And as I pulled it . . . the chicken took me!

So then I grabbed the leg.

Lifted up the chicken upside down.

In the meantime the chicken is struggling you know . . .

Because he not dead . . . right?

So he start struggling, flapping away . . . and I get scared.

Never having done this before, I grab by the leg.

I squeeze them together . . . and I wrap the cord just . . .

I didn't tie the leg.

I just wrapped the cord around the leg as much as I can.

Of course all of it was wadded up in my hand.

Anyway wrap . . . wrap . . . wrap . . . wrap . . .

So I look for something to lay this chicken on. And here was this cornbeef
box.

A case of cornbeef.

And they're not very large.

They're not very big, eh?

So I look at Jimmy.

I say, "Jimmy. Get that box over there for me."

So he brought the box.

I said, "Turn 'em upside down."

And when he put the box down . . . he put it down . . .

I *threw* the chicken onto like that and I *slap* . . . you know like that.

But the chicken was so heavy . . . that the head was hanging over the other
side . . .

And the leg was hanging down this side on the ground.

Well, I said, OK.

So . . . wait . . . wait . . . wait . . .

So I put my knee . . . one knee on the legs.

And then the other knee, I grabbed the wings . . .

And I tried to hold with one hand.

And my other knee I tried to brace myself on the box . . .

And same time grab the head . . . so I can twist the head back so I can expose the throat.

And I'm holding that chicken and I try to stay balanced on the box.

I tell Jimmy, "OK! Jimmy *now*!

Cut the throat!"

And I'm *waiting.*

And what I am noticing is that . . . when you lift up the chicken's throat . . . feathers stick out like that . . . and leave exposed you know . . .

I remember noticing how white the skin was.

And I'm watching that chicken.

"Go ahead. Jimmy, *Now! Now!*"

And when I looked up at him . . .

He's standing in front of me . . .

"No." He's forming the words, "no."

Well that darn chicken started to kick and struggle.

So I hold him.

I say, "OK. Give me the knife. Give me the knife."

So I switch position.

One knee on the legs . . . the other knee on the wings . . . and I'm holding the neck . . . and I went push like that . . . and when the knife went forward I could see . . . it just pushed the skin . . . it didn't cut anything . . . but when I pulled it back . . . I noticed the skin . . . just popped like a ripe tomato.

It just popped like that.

And there was coming . . . "*Ho my!*"

I remember staring at that.

All of a sudden . . . blood started gushing through.

All of a sudden I lost it.

I couldn't hold on.
And that chicken started to kick.

If I had known how to kill a chicken already the chicken would have died there.
But I didn't.
The chicken started to struggle.
I dropped the knife.
I even dropped the head.
And I struggled off the box.

Next thing I know, the chicken was standing up.
All the rope that I wound around his legs fell off . . .

And the chicken started to strut.
And cocky . . . how the rooster strut.
"Rrrp!"
And every time he went like that . . . the blood just spurt up like that.

"Hooo!"
So scared that all we could do was just stare at the dumb chicken.
He was supposed to be dead but he wouldn't die.
And he started walking toward the house!
Slowly walking toward the house.
When we figured out what was happening it was too late.
The chicken was *under* the house.

I said, "Jimmy! Jimmy! Go round side! Go round side!
Block up on the other side!
Then the chicken started *slowly* walking *way* to the bottom of the house . . .
On the end where the house rested right on the ground.
And when he couldn't walk upright anymore . . .
He just lay on the ground and push himself *all* the way into the edge.

And I when I look at that I say, "Awww, Kimo . . . go get 'im.
Go get 'im!"
He was on the outside.
But he say, "No . . . no . . . no . . ."

And I look at that . . . awww . . . that dumb chicken . . . all the way inside
  there.
So I just pysched myself up . . .
Cause all I could think of was . . .
Spiders . . .
Cockroaches . . .
Centipedes . . .
And scorpion.
Awww . . . cause all the webs hanging down . . .
And "woooow" I went under the house.
And I kept *staring* at that dumb chicken.
"Aawww . . ." Psyched myself up.
Just shut my eyes . . . and I started
Crawling underneath the house.

I went *all* the way inside.
Until I could feel . . .
I just reach hold . . . and I felt my hand on the chicken.
And I just pulled the chicken out.

Come back. I backed out so fast.
I just remember *throwing* the chicken on the ground and bouncing and
  kicking my feet and shaking all my body . . . so everything fell off.
And then when I look at that chicken . . .
The dumb chicken was dead.

I don't know why the chicken never die outside.
Instead of go all the way under there.

And then I hear . . .

"Makia! What you doing?
Makia! No *play* with that chicken!"

"No. Nancy. No."

Notes

1. Olivia Robello Breitha, *Olivia: My Life of Exile in Kalaupapa* (Pearl Harbor: Arizona Memorial Museum Association, 1998), 103–4.

2. Kalaupapa National Historical Park, nps.gov/kala/docs/history/htm.

3. The State Council of Hawaiian Homesteads Association, www.schha.com/dha.htm. For a downloadable film about the history of Papakolea, see www.filmworkspacific.com/papakoleavideo.html.

4. See Makia's written version of this story in Jack Canfield, Mark Victor Hansen, Sharon Linnéa, and Robin Stephens Rohr, *Chicken Soup from the Soul of Hawaii: Stories of Aloha to Create Paradise Wherever You Are* (Deerfield Beach, Fla.: Health Communications, Inc., 2003), 144–47.

5. Makia Malo, interviewed by Margaret Read MacDonald in his Kalaupapa cottage in November 1997. Two days of interviews, four tapes. Tapes in possession of interviewer.

6. Compare this 1997 version to the version edited from Makia's *Tales of a Hawiian Boyhood* audiotape in Eric Chock, James R. Harstad, Darrell H. Y. Lum, and Bill Teter, eds., *Growing Up Local: An Anthology of Poetry and Prose from Hawaii* (Honolulu: Bamboo Ridge Press, 1998), 77–80.

Bibliography

By Makia Malo

Malo, Makia. "Katie's Store." In *Chicken Soup from the Soul of Hawaii: Stories of Aloha to Create Paradise Wherever You Are,* ed. by Jack Canfield, Mark Victor Hansen, Sharon Linnéa, and Robin Stephens Rohr, 144–47. Deerfield Beach, Fla.: Health Communications, Inc., 2003.

———. *Makia: Tales of a Hawaiian Boyhood; The Kalaupapa Years.* Cassette tape. © Makia and Ann Malo, 1993. 581 Kamoku Street, #1804, Honolulu, HA 96826.

———. *Makia: Tales of a Hawaiian Boyhood; The Honolulu Years.* Cassette tape. © Makia and Ann Malo, 1994.

———. "The Rooster." In *Growing Up Local: An Anthology of Poetry and Prose from Hawaii,* ed. Eric Chock, James R. Harstad, Darrell H. Y. Lum, and Bill Teter, 77–80. Honolulu: Bamboo Ridge Press, 1998.

About Makia Malo

Dawrs, Stu. "Triumph of Laughter." Photos by Monte Costa. *Hana Hou! The Magazine of Hawaiian Airlines* 5(4) (August/September 2002): 28–35.

About Kalaupapa

Breitha, Olivia Robello. *Olivia: My Life of Exile in Kalaupapa.* [Honolulu]: Arizona Memorial Museum Association, 1988.

Jarrett, Roberta M. *Gifts from the Shore: A Kalaupapa Diary.* Illus. by Katherine Trnka. Beverton, Ore.: Pacific Editions, 1993.

Levin, Wayne. *Kalaupapa: A Portrait.* Photographs by Wayne Levin, text by Anwei Skinsnes Law. Honolulu: Arizona Memorial Museum Association and Bishop Museum Press, 1989.

Roos, Ann. *Man of Molokai: The Life of Father Damien.* Illustrated by Raymond Lufkin. Philadelphia: Lippincott, 1943.

Stewart, Richard. *Leper Priest of Moloka'i: The Father Damien Story.* Honolulu: University of Hawai'i Press, 2000.

Won-Ldy Paye. Photo courtesy of Won-Ldy Paye.

6

Won-Ldy Paye
A *"Play Person"*

If you can handle *your crowd . . .*
if you can play *with it . . .*
so the audience sees you have the fun.
WON-LDY PAYE

BACKGROUND NOTE ON LIBERIA

The West African country of Liberia lies on the Atlantic Ocean, bordered on the coast by Sierra Leone and the Ivory Coast and inland by Guinea. Liberia was established as a republic in 1822 as a result of the American Colonization Society's efforts to repatriate slaves to Africa. During the next forty years, more than twelve hundred slaves were relocated. Today, their descendants make up about 5 percent of the population. The rest of the population is made up of native groups: Kpelle, Bassa, Gio (Dan), Kru (Kro), Grebo, Mano, Krahn, Gola, Gbandi, Loma, Kissi, Vai, and Bella. In 1980, a military coup ousted President William R. Tolbert Jr., and since then the country has been plagued with constant civil wars. In August 2003, the latest dictator, Charles Taylor, went into exile, and Gyude Bryant took the reins. Monrovia, the country's capital is a city of approximately 1.35 million, more than a third of the country's estimated population of 3.3 million.[1]

Approximately 350,000 Dan live in the forests of the Nimba Mountain Range in northeastern Liberia and the western Ivory Coast. This is inland, away from the coast. Dan grow rice, cassava, and vegetables and supplement this with fish from streams. They farm coffee and rubber for market. Dan wooden sculpture is highly prized among art collectors.

Won-Ldy's hometown of Tapita is one of the largest Dan towns, located at the crossing of two of Liberia's main roads—the road from Monrovia, Liberia's capital on the coast, toward the Ivory Coast, and the road that runs from Guinea to the port of Buchanan.[2] The Dan are also known as "Gio" but prefer the term "Dan," as "Gio" derives from the Bassa phrases meaning "slave people."[3]

Meet Won-Ldy Paye

Won-Ldy Paye is a Seattle-based storyteller and drummer. He teaches dance and drumming and directs the performing group Village Mask and Drum, popular at festivals in the Northwest. Won-Ldy came to Seattle in 1988 and, for political reasons, is still unable to return to his home in Liberia. Won-Ldy talks about the importance of the storyteller in his native Dan society and shares his own performance techniques here.

Won-Ldy grew up in the Liberian town of Tapita. Though the town held around eight thousand inhabitants, much of Won-Ldy's young boyhood revolved around the compound of seven or so houses where he and many of his relatives lived and at the farms that his family prepared each year on the property of his aunt, Mami Gbandeh. Won-Ldy's maternal grandmother, Gowo, was of Dan descent and came from a line of storytellers. Both she and his aunt Mami Gbandeh carried on these traditions. It was important to these women that Won-Ldy and his brothers also learn the family art. Won-Ldy's father, who was Kro, came from a line of drummers, so Won-Ldy was also trained in that art form. In Won-Ldy the skills of drumming, dancing, and storytelling combined to create the *tlo-ker-mehn,* or play person. This art form surrounds story with multiple arts in performance.

Won-Ldy's storytelling skills won him public speaking and storytelling contests in his school years. At one point his skills landed him a TV role in a Liberian soap opera. Eventually, Won-Ldy formed a performing group, The Trow Trow Artists Workshop (*trow* means "play" in Dan). They presented health dramas on radio and on tour, with UNICEF sponsorship. When the group won a European award, Won-Ldy was given a fellowship to study Western theater and to lecture on African theater in the United

States. This brought him to Seattle on his first visit, in 1983. In 1988 he returned and has made his living as a performer and artist-in-the-schools ever since.

Talking with Won-Ldy

Won-Ldy's comments on storytelling are taken from interviews in 1991[4] and from taped lectures given by Won-Ldy at the 1994 National Storytelling Conference in Seattle[5] and at a Traditional Tellers Retreat held in 1987.[6] Added information comes from discussions between Won-Ldy and Meg Lippert during production of their book, *Why Leopard Has Spots*. Meg kindly provided transcriptions of those discussions.[7] And a few comments were taken from a panel discussion and interview at the Northwest Book-Fest in November 1999.[8]

A Storytelling Family

Won-Ldy came from a storytelling family. His grandmother was a griot. He told me that she would tell stories to him and his brother one evening and expect them to be able to repeat the tale back the next evening. Margaret H. Lippert asked Won-Ldy how he learned the art of storytelling:

> I come from a family of "Griots," storytellers. We tell stories when we work on the rice farm. At bedtime. Or when the kids get together. My grandmother would tell us stories every evening. Before Grandmother would tell her story, she might say, "Won-Ldy, it's your turn to tell a story." As I repeated the story, she and the other kids would correct me. After awhile I learned the stories and added my own style and fun and movement to them. By seventh grade, I was already telling stories to big crowds. People would say, "The kid's a good storyteller!"[9]

Speaking to me, Won-Ldy said of his storytelling family:

I am using the word now "storyteller" for the whole family . . . those who are engaged in storytelling. They are the people that the . . . people within the society look up to for a lot of things. They are the archives of the tradition. The storytellers are just regular people, you know, within the society. They are people themselves who take tremendous effort in their life to study that art of storytelling. Because, even though you are born in the family. Because you are a storyteller . . . you have to perfect your art. I mean you know *that* family knows it better than any other family. So you're not going to go to an outside family to teach you. So you have to perfect your own art.

So they spend a greater amount of time among themselves . . . every evening . . . or in the morning . . . or at work . . . telling stories to each other in all kinds of ways and forms . . . developing style.

The Storyteller's Role

The storytellers . . . they are the ones who are the archives of traditions. They must educate themselves to perfect their art. The storyteller represents a symbol of peace. Because you are political in a way. The storyteller is about the only one who can question authority without directly pointing a finger at the powers that be. For example the storyteller can talk about spider being a wealthy person and being corrupt. The storyteller will be talking about "spider," but it is really the chief who is corrupt. The chief himself will be sitting there, and the storyteller is talking about this corruption which is going on. But knowing that this is coming from the storyteller . . . that the storytellers are the defenders of the peace . . . people don't look at it as if they are trying to stir up problems. People feel that the storytellers are trying to *guide*. Trying to *guide* to what is *moral* within the community.

So if *you* are going to be the one who will set the value of things so people will be moral, then you must think yourself about your own actions. People expect a lot of calmness, a lot of self-control from people who are storytellers. Within myself, I try to live the same way too. I try to have a smile on my face all the time. Because I am the one who is always there, teaching kids. I am the one who is always telling kids . . . fighting is not good, cursing is not good, getting mad is not good. So if the kids see me getting mad, they start to wonder. Basically these stories have to do with morals.

So the storytellers in society possess all these qualities. And because of this, the people protect them. They are valued. They are catered to. Sometimes they even help them to make their farms. People trust them. They would leave their little kids with them, without any back-thinking at all.

The Function of the Teller in Traditional Arbitration

If you are that person, who the society depends on. You have to be responsible. If a storyteller was leaving to go to the farm, he would always tell people, "I'm going on the farm." Because if something happened while you are gone, they want to know how to track you down. Sometimes you are going out of the village. Then people have to approve of your going. Because what if something is going to happen while you are gone, what if a trial is going on? The storyteller is required on the jury. The storyteller sits on the jury but they don't make decisions. They just record the events. They don't *make* the decision. But they will be asked, "Have there been any situations like this that you recall? What happened then?" So the tellers will say, "Well, they were sitting right next to him like this . . . And based on this and this . . . it was solved *this* way." They would not say "Well, because you did this . . . this is your punishment . . ." They will only give a relationship.

The Storyteller as Historian in Traditional Society

A lot of the time in the villages the storytellers don't just look at themselves as performers. They look at themselves as historians. They are the people who carry the history of a tribe. And you don't just call them, "Come tell me a story!" They don't *do* that.

But they will always tell a story when a gathering is around. For instance, they might introduce the chief. The town crier will bring everybody to order and the first person to talk will be the storyteller. He will go on for five minutes or so, easing the people, making them laugh, and bringing the situation together, and *then* he will introduce the chief.

But again, if you look at what they are doing . . . they *are* performing. That's where the quality of a storyteller starts to take its place. Because if the storyteller is working with little kids . . . you've got to teach, but you're teaching must be adapted to more of a performance to be able to entertain little kids, in order for them to keep listening to you.

So the storyteller has to take up a new role. He can be a historian telling about history, or a performer telling to ten, twenty, or fifty little kids who might fall asleep! So what do you do to keep these little kids awake? You have to *perform* for them. You have to make them clap with you, you have to make them sing with you. And a lot of times you see yourself doing it with adults too. Because they get bored too. They are human beings just like kids.

THE ART OF STORYTELLING

So then we start to perform the *art*.
Now how do we perform the art is . . .
a couple of things start to happen.
You look at yourself as a performer because you want to get your message
    across.

So in order to get your message across . . .
you have to have *control.*
You don't want to come and create a loose situation that would spoil the
    act.
So from the time you stand up until the time you sit down,
you must *control* the audience.
So much *power* over the audience that when you get up there people look
    up to you not to bring about chaos.
So you have to bring that which is good.
For the betterment of society
or for the betterment of the reason for which you are standing to talk for.

With me, for example, every time I perform there is always a *big* smile
coming again. So this is the way I am getting adjusted, telling my audience
that I am happy because they are here.

Sometimes in the village you shake a couple of hands in the front. Or if
there are too many people and you can't shake all of their hands, you just
point your hand in front as greetings and they will point back. "Greetings."
And then there is a smile. You tell them you are happy to have them.

Some village storytellers will start by saying that they hope there is not an
enemy in the crowd. If there is an enemy, they would prefer to solve any dif-
ferences before he starts to tell his or her story. Because at that point, being
a symbol of peace, he prefers . . . no matter what the situation is . . . even
among a hundred people, he will tell the person, "Say it. Come up and say
it. Let me deal with it now."

Now. After you have set the stage with your audience,
that perfect decorum,
then you can perfectly continue your story.
So then, you start to entertain them.
When you start to entertain your people,
a storyteller must always have perfect pauses.
And to me a pause is not where you just keep quiet.
A pause is where a storyteller completely stops the story and asks some-
    one in the audience:
"How are you today?" "And you?"
"How did you hear about this event?"
And all of a sudden its like you forget about the story that is being told.
And you have to participate in the life of these people.
Make them feel that you *care* about the fact that they are there.

So one or two people answer you, and you say . . .
"Anyway . . . we will continue the story."
If you can handle the craft like *that*.
People always like to be *with* the storyteller,
because they feel that you are a brother or sister to them.
You are concerned about their well-being.
You are not just going to talk talk talk and go.

Pauses within the art of performance are unique to the storyteller. There are a lot of ways that storytellers do pauses. One way is to start a song. Tell everybody to sing. Not all stories have songs, but those that do, you can start the song, start the story, continue the song, come back to the story. But every story must have some kind of pause. You can't just continue on from beginning to end. If the story is *short?* Then you can just go on with it. But then, what is a short story? Based on how much control you have over your craft . . . I can extend a two-minute story to ten minutes. Easily!

I always say, "If you can do that . . . then *do* it!"
The audience *enjoys* that.
They like you playing with your art.
The art is like a puzzle.
It's like being on a checkerboard.
Being able to move from any direction to another.
And THAT is performing the story.
That is mastering your art.

Talking To Your Audience

Once you have been *talked* to you sit and listen. The person focuses their attention on *you.* When the person is *talking* to you, there is always that direct contact. You keep the person straight. Focused on *you.* So it is always better to talk to people. Get their attention. Call their name. Those are things you can do.

Movement

In the art of performing, another thing that I always do, I move. I am not just standing. I don't like to sit. 'Cause when I sit, it's difficult for the gesture to come about.
I like to . . . to rub my foot on the ground.

I like to . . . kick the air.
I like to . . . move my hands.
I like to . . . stretch myself.
I like to . . . yawn during the story.

I would do anything that I would do normally.
And I like to walk around.
Because when you are sitting watching me walk around, your head starts
    to move about.
If you see me waving my hands like this, it gets your attention.
So if you do some things like this,
it is easy to make one two-minute story take ten minutes.

All these are things in the *tradition.*
It is unique for we who are storytellers to observe these little things.
The movement.
The gestures.
The pauses.
Expanding a two-minute story to ten.
The songs that come in between.
Talking to the audience.
All those are part of storytelling.
Storytelling is a friendly conversation that you have with a group of
    people.
And it is really interesting to deal with that.

The Importance of Play in a Storyteller

In my tribe we say "*tlo-ker-mehn*" (*tró-ka-meh*). The word *tlo-ker-mehn*
means "play person." Then there is the *dano-pu-mehn,* which means "story
speak person." These are both from the Dan language.

I call myself *tlo-ker-mehn,* because if you look at me when I am perform-
    ing . . .
I am playing.
That is what makes people kind of admire me when I work,
because I *play* with the art.
When you are looking at me, you forget that I am talking with you,
it is like I am dealing with *myself.*

I am *there.*
I am playing by myself.
I am having *fun.*

The audience already have heard, Won-Ldy is a great storyteller. So they don't have anything bad about me. So when they come, they have already been way ahead of my being good. So I am left with just a little performance to do to prove it to them. I don't have much work to do. All I have to do is *play!*

And when the audience sees you enjoy yourself, they are convinced to go, "Well, I *like* him. He's having *fun.*" When they see you have fun with your art, they automatically start to have fun. So there's a philosophy I always say, "The audience enjoys me, because they see me enjoy *myself.*"

Sometimes I get onstage and I laugh to myself. I start to tell myself I'm going to have a great time here today. Sometimes I even tell the audience, "The reason I'm gonna have a great time is because there are a lot of funny stories and that makes me laugh a lot. I don't know why sometimes I laugh, but it's so funny that I can't stand it myself. So if you see my laugh, please bear with me. And then they start to enjoy that. Because it's rare for people to say, in front of an audience, "I'm here, I'm about to laugh." It's like I am admitting a fact. I will laugh, if it gets funny.

One of the acts that people used to *enjoy* about me in Liberia. I'd come and say, "I am coming to *lie.*" In the tribal tradition in West Africa, a lot of time they go, "Oh, those guys are *liars.* They know how to *lie.*" Because these things that you are formulating, they are based on one little thing. And you play with the whole art to make it a big huge thing. So just a little thing they know, but the rest surrounding it, they *don't* know. So they think you are lying simply because you are able to make a one-minute story into ten.

So I will come up and tell them, "I am about to lie to you. And I'm telling you straight. Because everything is going to be a lie. And by the time I'm done lying to you, you are going to admire me *so much.* And they *like to* hear that. I tell them *exactly* the way I'm going to have fun and what I'm going to do, and then when I explain and explain and then I start to talk to them, that is so *real.* I am telling them stories that are related to everyday lives. Even though I told them I was lying, I ask them, "Is this a *lie?*" They say, "No, that part is *true.*" I say, "No, that's not true. You *think* it's true because you are relating to that situation, but it's a *lie.*" And they get a kick out of that. "Oh yeah, he's lying. But everything he's saying is so *real.* Like it's *happening* in everyday life."

The Art of the Tlo-kro-mehn

The Dan people who are play persons are people who are *diverse* in the art. Almost all play persons do over ten different arts. But these are centered in the storyteller. They can dance, they can sing, they can play instruments, they can tell stories. But the whole thing is surrounded by story. *That* is *tlo-ker-mehn*. He is *not* just a storyteller.

That's another thing that you see in me. Sometimes I come onstage, a lot of times I tell only two stories. But the rest of the time all these other things are happening. So many things going on. I will play this instrument. I will jump from this instrument. I will make you do this. I quit doing that with you. I make you do this. We're *playing*. There is no specific toy there, but I can use the whole thing to *play* with. See, I'm using *words* as toys. I don't even need instruments to do that. I can make you play drums with your *mouth*. So I am playing the whole thing with you. So that's *tlo-ker-mehn*. That's the art of the *tlo-ker-mehn*. Being able to use everything in our environment.

The *dano-pu-mehn* is the straight story storyteller. He's a good performer too. But when you listen to him, you're hearing stories. Whereas when you listen to the *tlo-ker-mehn* he's manipulating you. He's doing all these things with your head. If the *tlo-ker-mehn* is around they say, "Watch your *clock*. If you have to leave after ten minutes you had better leave. Because he'll keep doing all of these things and you'll forget, you know."

Now if *you* can *handle* your crowd,
if you can *play* with it,
so the audience sees you have the *fun* . . .
the audience automatically starts to enjoy it.
That's the biggest secret about me performing.
When you watch me, you see it in my face, in the way I move.
Because what is funny is not determined by the audience,
you make it funny.
You say funny things so they laugh.
And because it *is* funny, *you* laugh.
So they enjoy the fact that you are happy.
And *that's* me.
That's the style *Won-Ldy*.
That's what people see in me.
When I'm up there . . .
one person . . .

Won-Ldy . . .
is going to have *fun!*

Won-Ldy's Story

THE DANCING BOOGEYMAN

Won-Ldy loves to dance and sing his boogeyman story. This is the way he per-
formed it at Bothell Library in August of 1991. Around two hundred children
and parents were gathered in a semicircle on the lawn. A friend drummed for
Won-Ldy while he told the tale.

Once upon a time *way out* in the village
there was a guy called Spider.
Sometimes they call Spider Ananse.
Can you guys dance?
This spider guy was a *great, great* dancer.
Do you think Won-Ldy can *dance?*
When it come to Spider dancing
ha . . ha . . Spider *real* good . . .
If you think you can dance
it's only because you haven't seen Spider.
He was the greatest dancer in the whole world.
When you say "Spider?"
they say "*Yeah. That* guy!"
Now there were these two boogeymen
they lived way out in the mountain.
They were jealous because Spider was a great dancer.
They don't like the idea that all the boys and girls in the village think that
Spider is a great dancer.

"We don't like this idea.
We gonna go to the village and show to the people at the village
that we can dance too."

"How we gonna go to the village? We are ugly."

The boys and girls run away from them.
Nobody see ugly boogeyman like that before.

"If we really got to go to the village . . .
Oh! I have an idea"! said one of the boogeymen.

"What's your idea?"

"We got to go to the tree.
The tree have nice flowers.
Flowers that smell real nice.
If we take the smell of the flowers . . .
we will be smelling real nice . . .
if we smell like the flowers . . .
everybody will like us!"

"That sounds good."

"But our voices are ugly.
We gonna borrow a nice voice from the bird."

"That's good too."

"There is one more."

"What's the other one?"

"Our skins are rough and ugly.
The snake has a smooth skin.
We gonna borrow that smooth skin from the snake
and when everybody see us, they gonna feel real happy,
because we gonna smell good and we got smooth skin.

Borrow the smell from the tree . . .
Borrow the skin from the snake . . .
Borrow the voice from the bird . . .
that way we can be . . . everybody gonna like us!

(*The boogeymen ask the audience*)
"What we borrow from the bird?"
(*Audience: voice*)
"What we borrow from the snake?"
(*Audience: skin*)

"What we borrow from the tree?"
(*Audience: smell*)

These two boogeymen borrowed these things, right?
So they looked exactly alike.
MAN if you think things look alike . . .
these guys looked SO much alike you couldn't tell one from the other.

When they got to the village,
One of the boogeymen went to hide behind the house.
So only one boogeyman was seen.

The chief said everyone in the village was going to come
for the great dance competition.

Only one boogeyman showed up.
This Spider and this boogeyman started to dance.
Everybody came around just like we got. (*indicating our audience*)

In the village, for the competition,
two persons would get in the middle of the dance floor
and they would dance until one person get tired.

You will get tired?
You the LOSER.
Everybody looking WHO are you.
They will THROW you away.

If you lose . . .

If you don't lose . . .
If you don't get tired . . .
Man . . . They lift you up and dance with you all around town . . .

You get lots of reward.

Dance competition starts.

(*Won-Ldy teaches song refrain to audience*)

"Gang gang pe." (*sound of boogeyman's footsteps dancing*)
Won-Ldy sings: "Tin y gepy."

Audience: "Gang gang pe."

Won-Ldy: "Tin y gepy."

Audience: "Gang gang pe."

(*We keep up the singing for a while, the drummer continues during the dance sequences of the story*)

Spider was dancing all over the place.
Everybody was singing the song.

"Tin y gepy!" "Gang gang pe!"
"Tin y gepy!" "Gang gang pe!"

Spider was dancing all over the place and now the boogeyman.

"Tin y gepy!" "Gang gang pe!"
"Tin y gepy!" "Gang gang pe!"

Spider was dancing . . . all over the sound.
"Tin y gepy!" "Gang gang pe!"
"Tin y gepy!" "Gang gang pe!"

Spider said, "This is a rough country.
I don't know who is going to win today.

'Cause he is a good dancer.
I'm getting tired.

"Tin y gepy!" "Gang gang pe!"
"Tin y gepy!" "Gang gang pe!"

(*confidentially*) Here is what was happening.
Every time when they were dancing.

"Tin y gepy!" "Gang gang pe!"

The other guy would go behind the house and switch.
with other one that look exactly like him.

Spider didn't know that.
Spider said, "How come?
He didn't have a problem himself?"
He's not going to win.
He really didn't like the idea that now the boogeyman is winning.

"Tin y gepy!" "Gang gang pe!"

"Geppy geppy!"
"Ti gepy!" "Gang gang pe!"
"Tin y gepy!" "Gang gang pe!"

He want to show to the people that he is the hero.

"Tin y gepy!" "Gang gang pe!"
"Tin y gepy!" "Gang gang pe!"

Boogeyman, they wanted to show to the village
that Spider would no more be the hero from this day.

"Tin y gepy!" "Gang gang pe!"
"Tin y gepy!" "Gang gang pe!"

A little brown bird flew down.
"Tin y gepy!" "Gang gang pe!"
"Tin y gepy! "Gang gang pe!"

He looked down on Spider . . . he said, "Boy I feel sorry for you."
"Tin y gepy!" "Gang gang pe!"
"Tin y gepy!" "Gang gang pe!"

He said, "You ought to follow that boogeyman."
"Tin y gepy!" "Gang gang pe!"
"Tin y gepy! "Gang gang pe!"

That gave Spider an idea.
He said, "I'm gonna follow that boogeyman from now on."

"Tin y gepy!" "Gang gang pe!"
"Tin y gepy! "Gang gang pe!"

He started following the boogeyman.
"Tin y gepy!" "Gang gang pe!"
"Tin y gepy! "Gang gang pe!"
Boogeyman turned to go behind the house.
Spider said, "No, I'm not going to let you go."
The boogeyman said, "Enough."
Boogeyman said, "Go away from us!"
Spider said, "No, I'm with the boogeyman."

"Tin y gepy!" "Gang gang pe!"
"Tin y gepy! "Gang gang pe!"

Boogeyman got tired. (*drum beat stops*)
(*rapidly*)
Boogeyman dance on his knees.
Knees got tired.
Dance on his stomach.
Stomach got tired.
Dance on his back.
Back got tired.
Dance on his shoulders.
Shoulders got tired.
Tried to dance on his head.
No way.

"Tin y gepy!" "Gang gang pe!"
"Tin y gepy!" "Gang gang pe!"

Spider started dancing all over the place.
He said, "You know you are going to fall down."
"Tin y gepy!" "Gang gang pe!"
"Tin y gepy!" "Gang gang pe!"

Awya Aw! Ya. (*groan; drum stops*)
Everybody see that this Spider wins.
Spider is the winner.
Everybody know that Spider is the winner.

Little bird whispers, "There's another boogeyman behind the house."
"WHAT!
I only get to see one boogeyman.
What do you mean there were two boogeymans?"

All of the people go and get the other boogeyman from behind the
house.
They got the other boogeyman.

In this village . . .
one of the biggest rules is "NO CHEATING," boys and girls.
They don't like cheating.
Anything you can do, you do the best you can do.
. . . to your best ability.

These boogeyman . . . took them WAY past the valley . . .
took them WAY over the mountain . . . took them WAY through
the swamp . . .
Threw them away.

You know what they did to the boogeyman?
They took them FAR from the village.
FAR from everyone.
And threw them away.
And since that day, boys and girls
in that land
you never see boogeyman.
Because the chief
THREW THEM AWAY.
So no matter where you go now . . .
in your home . . .
in the garbage can . . .
at school . . .
you NEVER see a boogeyman.
Because he threw them away.

You know why he threw them away?
Because . . . they cheat.
Because cheating is not good.
Yes?

(*song reprise*)
"Tin y gepy!" "Gang gang pe!"
"Tin y gepy!" "Gang gang pe!"

Notes

1. www.infoplease.com/ipa/A0107718.html.
2. Won-Ldy Paye and Margaret H. Lippert, *Why Leopard Has Spots: Dan Stories from Liberia* (Golden, Colo.: Fulcrum Kids, 1998), 38, 43.
3. D. Elwood Dunn and Svend E. Holsoe, *Historical Dictionary of Liberia,* African Historical Dictionaries, No. 38 (Metuchen, N.J., and London: Scarecrow Press, 1985), 55.
4. Won-Ldy Paye interviewed by Margaret Read MacDonald. Recorded on Capitol Hill Park lawn, fall 1991. Tape in possession of interviewer.
5. Lecture to storytellers at National Association for the Preservation and Perpetuation of Storytelling annual conference, held at the University of Washington, Seattle, July 1994.
6. Recorded at Traditional Storytellers Retreat in Fort Worden, Washington, fall 1991. Twenty-five listeners in living room of large home (officer's quarters). Session was repeated three times. Three tapes, with slightly different information. Tapes in possession of Margaret Read MacDonald.
7. Taped interview, Won-Ldy Paye and Margaret H. Lippert, June 19, 1991. Tape in possession of Margaret H. Lippert.
8. Comments during panel discussion at Northwest BookFest, November 1999, recorded by note-taking. Audio-recorded interview with Won-Ldy Paye was conducted by Margaret Read MacDonald this same day.
9. Won-Ldy Paye interviewed by Margaret H. Lippert, June 19, 1991. Tape in possession of Margaret H. Lippert.

Bibliography

Paye, Won-Ldy. *Won-Ldy Paye: Children's Stories.* CD. Seattle: Village Drum & Masquerade Productions, 1991.

Paye, Won-Ldy, and Margaret H. Lippert. *Head Body Legs.* Illustrated by Julie Paschkis. New York: Simon & Schuster, 2001.

———. *Hen and Crocodile.* Illustrated by Julie Paschkis. New York: Simon & Schuster, 2002.

———. *Why Leopard Has Spots: Dan Stories from Liberia.* Illustrations by Ashley Bryan. Golden, Colo.: Fulcrum, 1998. Includes background information about Won-Ldy's culture.

See also Won-Ldy Paye's website, www.wonldypaye.com.

7

Léonard Sam

I Try to Tell It Like My Grandfather

You can tell a story. But not without listening first.
Léonard Sam

Background Information: New Caledonia

New Caledonia (Nouvelle-Calédonie) is located in the South Pacific, 1,500 kilometers northeast of Australia and 1,700 kilometers north of New Zealand. The main island, *Grande Terre,* is one of the largest islands in the Pacific. Together with several outer islands, the country's total land mass is 19,103 square kilometers. New Caledonia became a French possession in 1853 and remains so to this day. A referendum on independence in 1998 did not pass. Another referendum is scheduled for 2014. New Caledonia's 210,789 inhabitants (July 2003) are divided into Melanesian, 42.5 percent; European, 37.1 percent; Wallisian, 8.4 percent (from Wallis Island); Polynesian, 3.8 percent; Indonesian, 3.6 percent (French citizens, turn-of-the-century immigrants); Vietnamese, 1.6 percent; and other, 3 percent. The literacy rate is 91 percent.[1]

The Caldoches, or white New Caledonians, are mostly descended from French convicts. The French used the area as a penal colony. These Caldoches have their own culture, rural in lifestyle. More recent French immigrants are called Métros and reside in the city.

The country's original inhabitants, the Kanak, are Melanesian. More than twenty-seven different Kanak languages are in use in New Caledonia. The Kanak culture centers on the clan and on *la coutume*— the code of rituals, social interaction between clans, and relationships with ancestors.

Léonard Sam. Photo courtesy of Léonard Sam.

Meet Léonard Sam

I was fortunate to hear Léonard Sam telling tales at the Glistening Waters Storytelling Festival in New Zealand in 1993. Though he told in French or Kanak, Léonard's engaging style drew us all into the story. Léonard is a professor at the Université de la Nouvelle-Calédonie in Nouméa, the capital of New Caledonia, where he supervises a diploma program called DEUG langues et cultures régionales. Léonard tells frequently in museums and schools in New Caledonia. Having learned the stories from his own grandparents, he is determined to keep them alive among today's children. He tells in French because he must use that language to be understood, but he also loves to share in his native Kanak. He feels that the stories can be done justice only in their original language. And he tells me there are twenty-eight different Kanak languages, without counting the many dialects!

Léonard agreed to let me interview him during a break in the festival in Masterton, New Zealand. The interview was given in French. I hope this translation captures the essence of Léonard's intent.[2]

On Telling in the Old Times

These stories were told in other times, in the traditional society, in the evenings, in the *case*. [French for a small dwelling or hut. The early Kanak *case* was round with a tall peaked thatch roof. Woven mats covered the floor.]

Everyone came together.
After the work in the fields or at fishing was over.
In the evening, everybody found themselves in the *case.*
This was the house. The *case.* The round *case.*

In the *case* there is one side for the grandparents.
And one side for the parents.
And in the middle, in the depth of the *case,* are the children.
It is here that they heard the great words.

In the evening the grandfather tells,
Or the grandmother tells the stories.
And the children ask of the grandparents,
"Grandfather, tell us a story?"

Then the grandfather tells.
But, there is a formula.
To begin the story, the grandfather says,
"Önië!!" (*Pronounced "Euh-ni-èhhh," sung with a falling off at the end*)
The children reply: Öi!! (*Pronounced "Euh-iiiii," responding in the same
    falling-off tone*)
Then the grandfather tells.

One cannot tell in the daytime because they say,
there is a popular belief,
that if one tells during the daytime one will become bald.
If you are telling stories . . . that is a pastime.
You work during the day.
So you wouldn't tell stories then.

On the Function of Stories

The stories have many functions.
    The function of play . . . ludic.
    In other words for amusement or diversion.
    There are humorous stories . . . droll.

    But there are also stories of initiation.
    Education in the traditions.
    There are the morals.
    They give the explanations.

    Why is this thing here? Why is that thing there?
    Why is that the tree you eat?
    Why is that tree put here or there?
    The stories explain all that . . .
    to the children they explain many things.

The Demise of Story

The problem is that now they are expiring, the stories.
    Now there is no more *case*.
    In place of the *case* are the house or the villa.
    In the villa is the television.

So the children come into the house,
and watch the television.
And also the older folks, who should be telling the stories.
Are also watching the television.

And thus the stories begin to disappear.

But I heard stories when I was little.
Because when I was little, there were no televisions yet.

But my own children have television.
And the stories will be lost.

Storytelling Revival

But now I have noticed that there is going to be a return to stories.
    People are beginning to realize that something is lost.
    And people are beginning to tell stories.
    In the school . . .
    They are organizing story parties . . .
    in the educational institutions . . .
    at cultural centers . . .
    in the museums . . .

But it isn't at all the same thing . . .
as in the *case*.
Not the same ambiance.

And now the stories are not the same thing,
because they must be adapted.

Because before we could tell in our *language*.
Each region had its language.
And the people told in their own languages.

Now I tell in French,
because in the class there are different languages,
and the French is the language most clear.

In every area there is a different dialect and language
and when I go from place to place,
I tell first in my own language, Kanak.

But when I tell in the museum,
I tell in my language.
And afterwards I tell in French.

And I tell the people, "It's great if some of you understand now,
and everyone else can try to understand."
And then I will tell in French and they can see how much they really
    understood.

But if the story cannot be told in its original language, it has to be
    adapted.
Something is lost.

Learning Stories

I learned stories by listening to my grandfather and my grandmother.
    Because there was no professional storytelling in my society.
    Anybody who has heard a story can start to tell once they are older.
    "Can I tell a story?"
    "You can tell a story. But not without listening first!"
    One does not become a storyteller without listening before.
    It is because of that that people have gathered stories and written them
        down.
    That's been done.
    But its not the same thing to read a story . . . then *listen* to a story.
    So that somebody who has read a story and has never heard it before
    cannot tell it the way it should be told.

Because there is a manner of telling.
Because in the stories there are many songs.
And you have to know how to sing them.

*Leonard gives as an example a story about two brothers that contains a
    song.*
Deux frères ramassaient des fruits de mer sur le récif.

Le plus jeune s'ècria:
"J'ai trouvè un bigorneau! J'ai trouvè un bigorneau!"
Le plus grand dit alors:
"Il est à moi! Il est à moi! Je l'ai trouvè le premier!"
Et il mit le coquillage dans son panier.
Ils continuèrent à pêcher.

[Two brothers were gathering seafood on the reef.
The youngest cried, "I found a bigorneau! I found a bigorneau!"
The big one said:
"It is mine! It is mine! I found it first!"
And he put the shellfish in his basket.
They continued to fish.]

Le plus jeune s'ècria de nouveau:
"J'ai trouvè un trocas! J'ai trouvè un trocas!"
Le plus grand répondit:
"Non, c'est moi qui l'ai trouvé le premier!

[The little one cried again:
"I found a trocas! I found a trocas!"
The big one said, "No! It is I who found it first!"]

And it was always like this. Every time the little one found something, the big one claimed it. In a large hole the little one discovered a large open *bénitier*.

The big one claimed it again, but while trying to lift it out of the hole, he put his big toe into the *bénitier* and it closed. Then the little one began to sing to call the waves:

Fenu fenua ke lo ma usiwa
Ka le kale ti teee ehia!
(*A song to call in the large waves, not translatable into French*)

And so that little song right there . . .
if it were not written down, you would not know how to sing it.
So if you were telling that story, you get to that part . . . how do you sing it?
It's very important to have heard it.

So that's the oral tradition.
But it's true that now, with the change in the audiences,
the stories have to adapt and change.

A Story Example

But I try to tell like my grandfather.

This is the story of the grandmother that lived in the little house.
And her grandson lived also with her.

Behind the house there was a fig tree.
One evening the figs became ripe.

"If you go out and bring me a flying fox, I'll give you a fig."

So he went out with a bat and killed a flying fox.
And Grandma is so happy.

So she puts it over the fire to get rid of its fur.
It's a happy reward.

So the two things they are teaching is that you need to respect the elders
and you need to eat everything.

Léonard's Tale

FLYING FOX STORY

I asked Léonard to tell a tale in his grandfather's style. The story he told is a lap story for a grandparent to use with a small child. During the story, the teller picks up the child's arms, legs, etc., and shakes them. The tale ends with a tickling of the child.
This story can be told by a grandmother or a grandfather.
We will say a grandmother.
This story of the grandmother and a little child.
They live alone in the case.

Behind the case is a flying fox.
One evening the flying fox was caught,
And grandmother roasted it.
"Who's going to eat the shoulder?"
And the child says . . . "Meeee . . ."
"Who's going to eat the other shoulder?"
"Meee . . ."
"And the foot. Who's going to eat the foot?"
"Meee . . ."
"Who's going to eat the other foot?"
"Meee . . ."
"Who's going to eat the head?"
"Meee . . ."
"And the tongue?"
"Meee . . ."
(*slowly*) "Who ate the rump?"
"Meee . . ."
Now the intestines . . . were the most important part to eat.
And normally this was reserved for the older persons.
"Who is going to eat the guts?"
"Meee!"
There was nothing left for the grandmother.
And the grandmother says (*tickling the child*)
"And who is this is going to eat the guts! . . . and who is this is going to eat
    the guts!
And what am *I* going to eat!"

Notes

1. Central Intelligence Agency, *The World Factbook,* "New Caledonia," www.cia.gov/
cia/publications/factbook/geos/nc.html.

2. Léonard Sam, speaking with Margaret Read MacDonald in teller's break room during Glistening Waters Festival, Masterton, New Zealand, November 1993. Interview conducted in French. One story told in Kanak. Tapes of poor quality. Translation assistance
from Jennifer MacDonald. Two audiotapes, in possession of author.

Bibliography

By Léonard Drile Sam

Drile, Sam, and Lercari, Claude. *Ifejicatre: Hna Xom Thei Itre Qatr Me Qatre Foe/ Contes et Légendes de Lifou.* [Tales and Legends of Lifou.] Noumea: C.T.R.D.P., Langues Vernacularies, 1983. In French and Dehu.

Sam, Léonard. *Dictionnaire drehu-français (Lifou, Nouvelle-Calédonie): Suivi d'un lexique français-drehu pour débutants.* Nouméa: Centre Territorial de Rechereche et de Documentation Pédagogiques, 1995.

———. *Enseigner le drehu, langue maternelle, et enseigner le français langue seconde, aux enfants de Lifou en Nouvelle-Calédonie,* Paris: Mémoire de DEA, Linguistique Générale et Appliquée, René Descartes, October, 1991.

———. *Ifejicatre me pengön e drehu: Traditions orales de Lifou.* Textes écrits par feu le vieux Saihnye Kacoco. Recuillis par Maurice Lenormand. Améliorés, ré-écrits dan la nouvelle écriture et traduits par Léonard, Drilë Sam. Illus. par Marcko Waheo. Nouméa: Centre Territorial de Recherche et de Documentation Pédagogiques, 1994.

———. "La littérature orale kanak." In *Chroniques du pays kanak* (encyclopédie), tome 3, Editions Planète Mémo, 1999.

———. "La Nouvelle-Calédonie, un Territoire Plurilingue: Le bilinguiseme en Nouvelle-Calédonie." *Notre Librairie: Revue du Livre: Afrique, Caraïbes, Océan Indien* 134 (May–August 1998): 30–43.

———. "Le temps dans la langue drehu." In *L'homme et le temps, Actes du Colloque.* CORAIL, Université Française du Pacifique, 1990.

———. "Les langues de Nouvelle-Calédonie: Des modernisations aux réformes intentionnelles." In *La réforme des langues, dirigé par Istvan Fodor et Claude Hagège,* with Jacqueline de La Fontinelle and Claude Lercari, 4:288–98. Hambourg: Buske, 1989.

———. "Les langues kanak dans le système éducatif." In *Education, Culture et Identité, Actes du Colloque.* CORAIL, Université Française du Pacifique, 1997.

———. "Les langues maternelles et l'école." In *Nouvelle-Calédonie: Problèmes et perspectives. Mémoire de maîtrise,* Paris III, et de Diplôme de Recherche et d'Etude Approfondie. Paris: INALCO, 1986.

———. "Pour une didactique des langues kanak." In *La France et les Outre-Mers, L'enjeu multiculturel,* with Claude Lercari. Paris: Hermès, CNRS Editions, 2002.

———. *Recuel de contes et légendes océaniens: Textes issus des concours de contes bilingues en langues océanienes organisés par le vice-rectorat.* Publication sous la responsabilité de Léonard Sam. Illus. de Marcko Waheo. Nouméa: Centre de documentation pédagogique, 1999. [Langues canaques 18]. [Collection of Oceanic Tales and Legends: Texts Issued from the Bilingual Contests of Tales in Oceanic Languages Organized by the Vice-Chancellorship.] Nouméa: Vice-Rectorat, Mission Langues et Cultures Régionales: Centre de Documentation Pédagogique, 1999.

———. "Vernacular Languages and Education in New Caledonia." In *Pacific Languages in Education.* Institute of Pacific Studies, Suva, Department of Literature and Language, Suva, Pacific Languages Unit, Vanuatu, 1996.

Lercari, Claude, D. Sam Léonard, Marc Gowé, and Jacques Vernaudon. *Langue de Lifou + Qene drehu: Méthode d'initiation*. Nouméa: Centre de documentation pédagogique de Nouvelle-Calédonie, 2001. [Langues Kanak]

About Kanak Folk Literature

Works about Kanak storytelling are written mainly in French. One interesting collection to examine is *Littérature orale: 60 contes mélanésiens de Nouvelle-Calédonie*. Nouméa: Société d'études historiques de la Nouvelle-Calédonie, 1980.

For an extensive bibliography of New Caledonian folklore texts see, http://members.tripod.com/~THSlone/PNGFB-New-Caledonia.html.

Lela Oman. Photo courtesy of George Sobo.

8

Lela Kiana Oman
They Are Preserved

Because people told these stories to me. They passed them on. And when I put them in writing, they are in writing for the first time. And they are preserved.
Lela Kiana Oman

Background Information about Nome

Nome is located on the Seward Peninsula, which juts out into the Bering Sea. Nome is 539 air miles northwest of Anchorage and 102 miles south of the Arctic Circle. Average snowfall is 56.2 inches per year. The shortest day of the year is December 21 (the winter solstice), with three hours and fifty-four minutes of sunlight. The daylight increases by approximately six minutes a day until June 21 (summer solstice), when the sun is up for twenty-one hours and thirty-nine minutes. Technically, the sun does set, but its close proximity to the horizon gives the appearance of twenty-four hours of daylight from mid-April to mid-August. Interestingly, though Lela has memories of winter storms, one of her strongest frightening memories is of sunstroke when she fell asleep in her tent during the summertime.

The 2000 population of Nome was 3,505—58 percent Alaskan native and 42 percent nonnative. The greater Seward Peninsula had a population of 9,196, with several small villages.[1]

The Inuit people residing on the Seward Peninsula and on King and Diomede Islands are Inupiat. They are related to the Central Yupik, who reside south of Unalakleet; the Siberian Yupik on St. Lawrence

Island; and the Chukotka people of Russia. Our teller, Lela Oman, prefers to use the term "Eskimo." She tells me that "Inuit" means "outhouse" in her language. Lela refers often to the relationship between her people and the peoples of the Russian side of the Arctic Circle.

Meet Lela Kiana Oman

Lela was born in 1915, the seventh child of Jim and Emma Kiana. Her family was from the Kobuk Valley area, and her father was of shamanic heritage. He moved to the new village of Noorvik so that his children could attend school. Lela heard many tales as a child. Some shared informally, father to daughter, and others shared in serious secrecy, the important legends that the missionaries now banned. "If we tell stories tonight, don't spread them around. Don't tell people about them," he warned. "Because then you will be known as children of sin." As a teenager, Lela heard stories from her aunt Susie Kiana Lockhart. Her aunt Susie had lived in several animals forms before finding her mother and being born as the human, Susie Kiana. She told wondrous tales.[2]

As a young mother, Lela Oman wrote down her culture's stories for the sake of her own children. But through the years her commitment to this work of preserving the tales of her people has grown into a nearly full-time job. In 1959, her *Eskimo Legends,* an unusual collection of mystical histories, was published by the Nome Publishing Company. By 1975, it had been discovered by the Alaska Methodist University and was republished by its press.

Meanwhile, *The Ghost of Kingikty and Other Eskimo Legends* had been published in 1967. In 1995, the Carleton University Press and the University of Washington Press copublished the *Epic of Qayaq: The Longest Story Ever Told by My People.* Some parts of this epic had been written down in the 1940s while Lela ran a roadhouse in the mining town of Candle, Alaska. In the evenings the Inupiat miners would share tales, and later Lela would write down what she had heard. Much later, in 1975, she pulled out those notes and combined them with memories of her own family members' tellings to piece together the entire epic.

Talking with Lela

I interviewed Lela at her son's home in Snohomish, Washington.[3] I had met her at a Traditional Teller's Retreat at Fort Worden State Park. Lela had come to the retreat as a participant, probably thinking it was a retreat *for* traditional tellers, rather than a retreat for teachers and librarians to *meet* traditional tellers. The next year, we invited Lela to return as a featured teller. In her presentations, she told very little but talked a lot about her culture. Likewise, in our several interviews, Lela told me much about her childhood and her culture but shared only a few stories. She sees her function perhaps as a preserver of tales to print rather than as a performer.

The interviews took place during three visits in February of 1992 while Lela was escaping the Nome winter with a visit to her son. Lela's son works for the Boeing Company and owns a large new home in the foothills of the Cascade Mountains. I interviewed Lela at their handsome dining room table with mountain views and luxurious suburban homes in view.

I ask Lela how she got started on this arduous task of writing down the stories.
    Well, it just was natural for me . . . because I am a descendant of storytellers.
    And while I was doing those two books, I was doing other things . . . like running for this . . . running for that . . . being on a committee for this and that, you know . . . and raising my five children, along with my twenty foster children.

    It was natural for me. Because my people were Kobukan people.
    And they were the people that owned the Kobukan Valley[4] at one time.
    They were the chiefs . . . and the rich people.

Lela talks about how some stories were told over many nights.
    And this one here . . . the longest . . . and the oldest story ever told, was
        told in the community hall. A very big hall . . . at that time. So many
        people . . . This here. It was told by Eskimos. It's known by *all* the Eskimos around the circumpolar. And each one telling it their own way.
    Right around the Kobuk Valley they wait for the shortest day of the year.
    Which would be around December. Coldest and the shortest days.
    That's when hunting and going after things . . . is real hard.
    And they usually had the storyteller, usually somebody that is a chief,
    or from Kobuk Valley you would say. And then since the stories are *so*
        long,
    the storyteller stayed quiet . . . long enough to sleep . . . or eat.
    And people are waiting on him.

    And some people say they did it just in the evenings.
    But, they waited for the *shortest* days of the year,

which are usually the month of December.
The shortest days of the year are around four hours.

But the other twenty hours in the day would be evening. You could be telling?
Yes. And then they told them in their community halls.
These community halls are usually *great* big round dugouts.
They are framed with trees.
And then covered with sod and mud.
Nice and warm.
And then there's always a hole up there.
They call it the "smoke hole."
And there's an open fire in the middle.
People . . . can do their celebrations . . . and dances . . .
and they are big enough to take in the whole village.
They can take in the whole village.

Tell me more about hearing stories. When you were a child, did you hear stories from your father? Your mother?
Mmhmm. My father. My aunt.
And other older people.
And when we were growing up they were real strong Christians.
And the missionaries looked upon storytelling as a sin.
You are turning back.
And you must never look back.
And we grew up on the Quaker faith.
Went to church.
And they are still following that same system.
Right now.
Not as strong as it was when we were children.
If we went to talk Eskimo, we were punished for it.
And the ministers that came up were also teachers.
And they were sent up by the government to our area.
And then, at first, when they first saw dancing . . . Eskimo dancing?
Some of them were trying to learn to dance.
Until they *saw* what really happens . . . what really happens . . . under
    that . . .
(*Lela mimes the slow, mesmerizing beat of the drum*)
. . . influence of the drum.
And the songs . . . the old songs . . .
because they were used to summon the powers.

Especially one . . . what they call the "Wolf Dance."
And after, they looked upon it as witchcraft and evil.
And right *now* they put a stop to it.

Because . . . through the drums and their songs
they summoned the powers
and these dancers had the wands . . .
that's what was happening.
Just before missionaries came around.

I asked Lela if people just forget how to do that then.
My father . . . one time I asked him. I talked to him about that. "Why we don't have the magic words? And they have those wands, that they use when they are performing. Why don't we have them anymore?"

And he said, "They still do. But we do not believe in them anymore. But they are still with us. But we have a different kind of religion now."

You said the shamans used to be able to cure people? Without any recuperation period, they would just be cured?
And my Dad had seen so much of it when he was growing up that he said . . . "Take the pill from the doctors. Works the same. If you believe in it."

I asked Lela when she first began collecting stories and writing them down.
When I first started it I thought I was just doing it for my children. They were little babies. I would tell them little baby stories. About a mouse going down to Kotzebue to get married. Or about the porcupine going across the river, you know.

But then I got to thinking. I have just got to put them down. Because there is the radio. And there was TV. And especially at Nome, just before I woke the kids up, my husband worked for the company, mining company, and had to go to work six o'clock in the morning. And from six o'clock in the morning up until eight, when I woke my children, so they could go to school, I had that length of time to myself.

And that's when I did quite a bit of it. And I was still quite young then. And then thinking I am doing it for my kids.

Oh, they will be in notebooks, and some of them in ledgers, cause we were in business too, before we moved to Nome. And especially that one [*Epic of Qayaq*] was in ledgers where I scribbled and scribbled and then the typist copied those ledgers. And then I still have those ledgers that I had been scribbling on in '47, '48. Especially that one I had to do quite a research on that. And then this *Ghost of Kingikty*. I knew of the story. My aunt told me the story. And after I wrote the story I went to be with a lady that was from Wales.[5] And I had her tell me that story.

Sometimes I will write down the story just the way I heard it. And then knowing somebody else knows about it, I will go and talk to that person. And that way I know I have done some research work.

But there are some that we know. That we have heard, ever since we can remember. A lot of people know of that story. All along the circumpolar. And I also wrote, briefly, every one that had told me. And then on top of that, I had known about it long before I knew these storytellers. I would talk to somebody and then the next day I would write it down. And my husband would say, "Are we going to keep an extra girl in the restaurant there?" And I would say "Better. Because I still have that much to write."

> It costs us something, you know.
> But I had it done.
> And I tried my best to keep it *just* the way I heard it from the old people.
> And it was so very hard from me.
> Because I had to translate it from the Eskimo to English.
> Now, I am so used to translating from Eskimo to English . . .
> now translating back to Eskimo again . . . that's harder yet!

I ask if the folks who told her stories were storytellers or just folks who happened to know the stories.

> They happened to know those stories.
> They had absorbed them as they were growing up.
> And then telling them to others.
> Especially those that asked.
> And I was one of these.
> Just because I was putting them down.
> And they knew that I wanted to tell.
> They knew that I was writing them down.
> And that's what made it so interesting.

When we first moved to Nome, I knew quite a lot of women friends from different villages. That I went to school with. And they would come and visit me. And before I know it . . . somebody's telling us a story. And that was *so* interesting to me.

And that was very beneficial too. Because I would have that story . . .
already written . . . what I came out with . . . what I had absorbed from
somebody . . . I am writing it . . . then another [version] too.

And then another thing that I had made myself do. Not to try to change
their stories. From their point of view. No matter how strange it seemed to
me. Only to try and keep them just the way the natives told the story.

So your friends might tell stories without you asking them? Just sharing . . .

Sharing stories . . . like for instance in the evening we'd be having a cup of
tea, or spending an evening together, especially visitors from villages, and
they were very interesting. Now those people that have done that are gone.
They died off.

And each and every person that I had gotten the stories from are gone.

*Lela is working with another scholar now to translate some of the stories back
into Eskimo. Her friend took her to Belize for a working vacation.*

That was a tough one. That's why we had to go down to Belize. And get
away from anywhere. So we could work on it. We got into some arguments
too. I was warned. On that too. Like . . . I have been on my own . . . a long time.
Doing things on my own. My own words. Without anybody coaching me.

> And then a writer that had lived in the University of Alaska . . .
> having these doctors tell her what to do . . .
> straightening it out . . .
> straightening it out . . .
> she told me . . .
> "Whatever you do, stay away from them!
> They polish it so much . . .
> that there is no more true truth left
> and no more beauty in them anymore.
> And they turn things around their *own* way."
> And that's what she told me.
> She warned me against that.

And then when I was working with Priscilla and Maree[6] . . . I understood
that. But there were things that had to match. Like this part here . . . I wrote
it out . . . according to the way my uncle told it. Knowing the story so well
. . . I would straighten something out. And it didn't jibe with *these* Eskimos.
And then they started warning me about the doctors that would be seeing

that. I said, "See here. These doctors . . . these university doctors . . . have been using my work for many years . . . without my permission. And I've been willing to . . .

We got into arguments now and then. (*Lela chuckles*) I had to. Hold my ground too. Mmmhmm. But then . . . we worked it out together.

Her linguist friends have used a German system of notation to transcribe.

They wanted it to be different. They wanted it to be different from any other language. That's why they left it like that. They have done this kind of work for people all over the world.

Lela talked about her one hundred-year-old uncle Ed Norwig who "looked just like a Norwegian." She explained that a group of Norwegians had been ship-wrecked about six hundred years ago and traveled until they reached the Kobuk River valley. "And they settled there, just to spend the spring. And they never left."

Lela is fascinated with the various cultural connections of her valley. One of her own ancestors was, according to tradition, a Hawaiian sailor named Kiana. She has contacted folks in Hawaii and is trying to trace this ancestry.

Lela also tells a fascinating story about people from her area magically fly-ing to Russia once upon a time and bringing back iron objects that are still found in sites. She had heard the story from a lady from Shisharoff, Alaska, which is on the coast and not that far from Siberia. At that time there was no metal on the Alaskan side of the Arctic Ocean. The person who flew to Siberia brought back a metal saw.

And it was a *big* one.
And there was *Nooooo* kind of metal.
On the Alaska sound.
So they cut the saw into *tiny* pieces
and made needles out of it.

And then . . . somebody else
under the same power.
Went over there and brought home . . .
big . . . iron pieces.
And she describes them as heavy . . .
and sort of something like a staff . . .
And they had little holes . . . and they thought like . . . might
be part of like a ship . . . where the holes were might have

been where nails . . .
And after they brought both those iron pieces home they didn't
know what to do with them.
So they just let them lay there.
And she told me . . .
if you happen to go over there you could see them.
They probably *are* thrown away . . .
or under the ground by now
because growth, growth covers things.
But she, she said she saw them.
European . . . and how they came across from Siberia side.

Lela's father told many stories when she was a child.
He told us *sooo* many stories.
And see these people that . . . raised their children by hunting . . .
did not have to . . . follow the clock.
Didn't have to . . . go and work for somebody . . .
bringing . . . food off the country . . .
making a living off of the country.
And . . . that was hard living.
It's *always* uncertain.
It's really tough living.

Still we were *free.*
Living on the beautiful country.

And he would tell you stories in the evening time?
When we would go to bed.
We are in bed.
And sometimes when it was raining too.
He would tell us stories when it was raining
to keep us still.

And then also in the wintertime . . .
we don't see those kind of storms anymore.
We used to be in the . . . just right between so many high mountains . . .
high mountains that were toward Kobuk . . .
and high mountains over towards the other side.
And it is a basin.

And the wind, strong wind gets in there . . . and it goes around until it
stacks up.
And sometimes it lasts for a whole week.

And we would be inside that cabin for a whole week.
The only person that we would hear . . . from the window it'd be my
uncle.
Making sure that we were all okay.
He would talk to my father and my father would say, "We're fine . . ."
And sometimes we would let the dogs go for a couple of days without
feeding them, because they were better off covered up there.
My father used to say, "We're not going to disturb them.
It's *too* hard. To listen to them after we feed them."
And when that happens they wouldn't feed them anything warm.
They have to feed them something that is frozen.
Would be frozen fish.
And the dogs are eating that frozen fish.
And some of them bit down real fast but sometimes there would be a *dog*
screaming out there.
That means it is *sooo* cold he is screaming, and it takes him for a while to
settle down. And we *always* know by the sound whose dog that is.
Oooohhh it's so pitiful.
But then . . . when it quiets down we know that it curled up.
And then frozen fish . . . that they eat seemed to push that warmth out.
And then the frozen fish that's cooked inside their stomach it gives them
strength.
Even . . . some people have done that.
If they are very cold they take something cold, to push the warmth out.
And then they feel better afterwards.
You don't see that kind of thing anymore.
And besides we have outside help.

*Lela explains that they lived in a log cabin at that time. In the summer they
would live in tents to be nearer the river.*
At Nervik our log cabins were high up on the ridge.
So it was better for us to be right down there next to that water in tents.
And Kobuk River can get *so* hot.
When it was *so* hot in summertime it could reach 114.
Last summer in *Nome,* it even reached 111.

When it was *real* hot on the Kobuk, they would tell us never to go to sleep
   in our tents. Because if you go to sleep,
and the sun is still hot through that tent, through the canvas . . .
and they didn't *know* that I was asleep in that tent.
It was awfully easy to go asleep.
And they didn't know that I was in the tent . . . asleep.
When I woke up here my nose was bleeding.
Everything I saw was pink.
Even the light pink. I couldn't distinguish anything.
Everything was pink.
I guess I had a sun stroke one time and that's why I can't take it.
When it gets *so* hot up there.
Our mukluks often make us wade around in the water.
To cool off.
Would you be wearing your mukluks when it was that hot!
We never went barefoot.

*I asked Lela if the various kinds of stories had genre names. Bedtime stories?
Legends? Lela explains that the legends weren't thought of as folktales at all but
as historical accounts. Lela was raised in a family with a Christian heritage,
which means they are not supposed to accept the legends as truth anymore.*

Well we think of them as legends now. At that time when they really had
happened, it was during the time, they always say, when our mother nature
was bad. They thought of this . . . mother nature was bad. Well that is the
religious way. Like we had no religion then. We refuse to believe in things
like that anymore. But my father said, "Respect them. That's all we had at
one time."

And now that I have worked on the Kobuk Valley history. That is my
background. That is not legend. Those things are true. Are history. But still
so many things have happened to them too. Like disappearing and then
appearing, just like in the Bible times.

*I asked for a story I had heard Lela tell at a conference one time. "Can you tell
me the one about going to Kotzebue to get married? Can you tell me a story like
that?" Lela chuckles and begins.*

And that is the favorite story of my mother's . . . to the babies. And then
. . . especially when the child is . . . kind of active . . . maybe about two years
old . . . three years old.

It's a mouse.

MOUSE, MOUSE

A mouse . . .
was going down to Kotzebue on Kobuk River.
And they were *so* happy
because a little girl mouse . . . was waiting for him to Kotzebue.
And he heard a voice from the willows saying,
"Mouse . . . Mouse . . . where are you going?"
And the mouse said,
"I am going to Kotzebue to get married."
And the voice from the willows said,
"Don't go where it is *deep*.
You be very careful.
Don't go where it is *deep*."

And the mouse said,
"I wouldn't go where it is deep."

But he was *very* happy.
And he was swimming down the river.
And he forgot all about deep area.
And the little pike swallowed him.

And this . . .
this teaches . . .
that no matter how happy you are
you have to be *very* careful.

I exclaim in surprise, "And that's the END! Oh!" But Lela is chuckling.
But by the end the baby is *sound* asleep.
"Mouse. Mouse. *Aviññaq. Aviññaq.*
Where are you going?"
"I'm going to Kotzebue to get married."
Oohhh . . .
When you tell that story to the baby that is going to sleep . . .
Especially inside the tent and it is *dark* you know?
That is *so* real.

And would you string it out . . . like sing that over and over again?
Yes . . . and then the baby is still not asleep.
And then the mother has to tell it all over again.

"This little mouse . . . *Aviññaq* . . .
was going down Kobuk River.
And he heard a voice from the willows saying
"Mouse. Mouse. *Aviññaq. Aviññaq.*
Where are you going?"
"I am going down to Kotzebue to get married."
Because there was a little girl mouse waiting for him
down at Kotzebue.
And the voice from the willows said,
"You be very careful.
Don't go where it gets deep."
And the mouse said he wouldn't go where it gets deep,
but he was *very* happy.
As he was going down the river he forgot all about being careful.
And the little pike *swallowed* him.

And this has a moral:
That no matter how happy you are
you must be *very* careful.

Those are *very* entertaining.
'Cause we listen to them.

Do stories like that usually have a moral?
    Mmhmm. Told to kids.
    That no matter how happy they are,
    they must be *very* careful.
    We lived in a wild country.
    And these kind of stories taught us lessons.
    Like the chickadee bird . . .
    One day . . . a little chickadee bird and a mouse were playing.
    And the mouse got roughed up
    and tore the chickadee bird's parka.
    And the chickadee bird started crying.
    And she cried . . . "I am so poor . . .
    I am so poor . . .
    Now my parka is torn.
    He thought I was wearing a parka . . . just as thick as his.
    I feel *so* poor."
    And the chickadee bird *cried.*

And the mouse heard chickadee bird *crying.*
Peeked out from its nest
and listened to that crying.
And the mouse decided he was going to brag a little bit more.
He peeked out and looked at that chickadee bird that was crying.
And he hollered at the chickadee bird.
Picnigaya qa qa nqayahai.
Which means,
He's got grass roots . . .
and little sweet round growths that are on the ground . . .
round black things that are really sweet to eat.
And he must brag and tell this chickadee bird he has grass roots,
and those things to eat . . . inside his home.
Bragging . . . to that poor little chickadee bird that's crying.
The end.

Lela laughs. I ask her to explain the story.
You must *never* brag to somebody,
like the chickadee is *soo* sorry for himself.
Here is the little chickadee bird crying . . .
feeling *soo* sorry for himself.
Because even the parka that she was wearing
was not thick as the mouse's parka.
And she is crying, "I am so poor, I am so poor.
I am so poor, I am so poor."
The mouse heard this.
Decided to brag a little more.
Which means . . .
when you see anybody . . .
looking poorer than yourself,
don't let them know that you have.
You'll make them feel worse.
That's the moral to that.

So these stories were often examples of what you shouldn't do.
What you shouldn't do. Mmmhmm.
Because ooooohhh when my mother is telling that story . . .
it was sooooo . . .
inside there . . .
and it was *dark.*

And we're listening to that . . .
and you see the little chickadee bird . . .
and the mouse playing hard . . .
and then you see her going off to sleep . . .
you feel *soooo* sorry for that little chickadee bird.

You know these have . . .
These stories have an affect . . . on people.
These kind of stories . . . told to put children to sleep . . .
And we can fall asleep . . . talking about it.

Lela and I laugh because we are both lulling to sleep under Lela's story spell. I wonder, "Beautiful little stories. Would your mother ever then, if you were doing something, would she ever say to you, 'Remember little chickadee?' Or something like that?"
Well . . . they told these stories to us quietly.
Away from people.
And if we did something . . . in front of people,
they did not go after us in front of people.
Usually later, "That time you did that and that's *wrong.*"

I say to Lela, "Tell me another one. Do you have another one?" Laughing, I add, "If I don't fall asleep."
There are *so* many little animals that have talked.
They called them . . .
like in the Bible there are only two animals that talked.
And that's the serpent . . . and the donkey.
You remember that?
But in our stories . . . in our old stories . . .
a *lot* of things talked to people.
And even in their stories . . . something like Disney World . . .
and birds talking . . . and their songs . . . and telling people what can happen.
And there is one *real* good story . . .
that I *never* forgot.
"Achuqli."
Dad told that story many times.
We would learn to sing it.
"Achuqli chuli. Achuqli chuli."
That's what the bird, what it sang.

I asked, "Did you sing along with your father?"
    Sometimes we did.
    Because he told us *sooo* many stories.

When I thanked Lela for taking the time for our several interview sessions, she told me,
    Wherever I am needed . . . as a storyteller,
    or to help somebody,
    I always go after it.
    Because people shared these stories,
    and they orally passed them on to us.
    And when *I* put them in writing,
    they are in writing for the first time.
    And they are preserved.

Lela's Story

ACHUQLI

    And there is one *real* good story
    That I *never* forgot.

    And the name of that story is Achuqli.

    A man, named Achuqli, had a wife
    And two children . . . a boy and a girl.

    They were living away from people.
    Quite a ways from the seacoast.
    Among the mountains.

    And they had lived on . . . the bears . . . caribou . . .
    Whatever a man can bring home to live on.

    They had a *great* big cache next to their sod house.

    These big caches are off the ground and they are just like houses . . . on
        stilts . . . and they had one like that.

And there were animal skins in there.
There were wolf skins . . . and wolverine skins . . . and bear skins.

When this Achuqli kept going off to hunt,
he was beginning to stay away
more and more.

He would come home,
bring home food for his children and his wife.

And later on things got so that he hardly showed up.
Then one day he came home sick.
Not too long after he got sick . . .
He died.

And just before he died,
he told his wife to put wolf skin and a wolverine skin with his body.
And to wrap his body in . . .
at that time they wrapped the bodies in skins that had been used to cover
    boats.
That they had been wet . . . and dry . . . and wet . . . and dry . . .
Until they are just *real* hard.
And when a person died . . . they would wrap them in these.
And they encased in those . . . and kept dry . . .
And sometimes they mummified.

And when the spring came around,
the woman was sitting outside of her sod house.
And there is her husband.
Close by.
Off the ground on stilts . . .
Wrapping in mummy . . . I mean in that . . . skin.
And she was crying.
She was crying.
She looked at her husband . . .

Finally a *bird* landed close by.
And it was singing.
And the sound is

"*aachuqli . . . aachuqli . . . ii*
    Paniyavim panianik nuliaqtuq"

And the woman understood.
"*Aachuqli chuqli . . . aachuqli chuqli . . .*
He married Paniavik's daughter."

And that woman was *soooo* surprised.

She got that bird . . .
To see if it would sing again.

And there it was.

But her husband, Aachuqli chuqli was dead.
And there was his body.
Finally . . . she said to that bird.

"You fly . . . towards where my husband is."

And the bird took off.
Down towards the sea.
And that woman watched that bird.
And that bird flew over . . .
Sort of hills . . . close to where they lived.
Rolling hills . . . cause that's the way Alaska is . . .
Rolling hills . . . with no trees . . .
Went over the rolling hill . . .
And went over another one . . .
And she watched . . .
Until she could not see that bird.

And . . . she stood up and went over and examined that skin . . .
Where her husband was supposed to be in.
There it was empty.
The skin.
What was also missing with the body . . . was the wolf skin.

And when it had happened there must have been little bit of snow on the
    ground yet,

because it was springtime . . .
And she saw . . .
wolf tracks.
Leading towards where that bird had taken off.
She knew that her husband had tricked her.
'Cause the bird said that he had taken Paniavik's daughter for a wife.

And she went up to that cache . . .
Got down a female . . . bear's skin . . .
And two cub skins . . .
From the cache.

And she tanned them.

After she had tanned them . . .
She put one on.
Just to fit her.
And the cub skins that she had tanned . . .
She put them on her kids.
And when she put them on her kids,
the kids started getting *real* rough!
Running around.
Careless and *rough*.
And she had to take those skins off of them,
before they would hurt each other.

So . . . not too long after.
She knew what she had to do.

She had put a board . . .
At one time women always had a nice smooth board to cut their skins on.
She put her board where she cut skins right on her chest.
Covered herself with this.

And her two children . . . the boy and a girl . . .
Were in the bear skins.

And she took them towards the sea.
Where the bird had taken off.
Because she knew just where that bird had taken off toward the sea.

She walked and she walked a *loooong* time with her cubs.
And soon she heard noise made by villagers.
Men and women sounded like they were playing football.
At that time they'd kick a ball around,
and have goals . . . and they called it football.

And she climbed up a low hill and peeked over . . .
And she recognized her husband . . .
Playing ball among them.

There was a *beautiful* woman that was playing ball also.
And they would *chase* the ball . . .
And after a while . . . they would *embrace.*
And that hurt her *soooo* bad.

She got away from there and took her children behind a big flat stone.
And she got up on top of the hill and showed herself.
And those people that were playing football noticed her.
And they went to get their bows and arrows.
And she knew that her husband was a *very* strong, good hunter.
She knew that *he* was going to come for her.
Because she was a *bear.*

After she knew that her husband was with the others,
She led them away from the children.
She had told her children,
"No matter what happens . . . don't you come.
You just stay right here."

And sure enough . . . the others gave up.
And this man . . . that was her husband . . . still was chasing her.

Finally, when she noticed that he was all alone . . .
She got behind a stone and took her hood off . . .
And waited for him.

And he recognized her.
And he said, "Where are the children?"

That's how he said,
"Where are the children?"

And she said to him,
"You did not think of your children.
They did not mean anything to you."

And she put her hood back on.
And she killed him.
Because she was a bear.

And *many* years later . . .
Over the years . . .
All along that sea coast where this had happened . . .
They would see a bear
with two cubs.

And sometimes in wintertime they would see . . .
Tracks . . . of a mother bear . . .
With two cubs.
And they left them alone.

Because they knew.
Who they were.

And this is supposed to be a true story.
It is just the way they have told it.
Like when somebody is so hurt.
That they turn into something.
And revenge with somebody.

Akkumi.
Akkumi.

The end.

Notes

1. Statistics from www.nomealaska.org.

2. Selected data from Charles Wohlforth, "Lela Oman and the Epic of Qayak," *Anchorage Daily News,* "We Alaskans" section, April 20, 1997.

3. February 1992, home of Lela's son near Snohomish, Washington. Interviews by Margaret Read MacDonald. Tapes in possession of author.

4. Kobuk Valley National Park is encircled by the Baird and Waring mountain ranges. The park includes the central portion of the Kobuk River, the twenty-five-square-mile Great Kobuk Sand Dunes, and the Little Kobuk and Hunt River dunes. Sand created by the grinding action of ancient glaciers has been carried to the Kobuk Valley by both wind and water. Dunes now cover much of the southern portion of the Kobuk Valley, where they are naturally stabilized by vegetation. River bluffs, composed of sand and standing as high as 150 feet, hold permafrost ice wedges and the fossils of Ice Age mammals. See www.nps.gov/kova/.

5. Alaskan village.

6. Priscilla Tyler and Maree Brooks.

Bibliography of Lela's Work

Oman, Lela Kiana. *The Epic of Qayaq: The Longest Story Ever Told by My People.* Ed. Priscilla Tyler and Maree Brooks. Ottawa: Carlton University Press; Seattle: University of Washington Press, 1995.

———. *Eskimo Legends.* Illus. Minnie Kiana Keezer. Anchorage: Alaska Methodist University Press, 1975.

———. *The Ghost of Kingikty and Other Eskimo Legends.* Anchorage: K. Wray's Print Shop, 1967.

9

Peter Pipim

Fill It Up with a Song

You don't sit there and just listen. You are part of it.
When something is said which is exciting the story . . . you
want to fill it up with a song.
PETER PIPIM

BACKGROUND INFORMATION ABOUT GHANA, KUMASI, AND THE AKAN

Ghana is located on the West Coast of Africa, bounded on the coasts by the Ivory Coast and Togo and inland by Bukina Fasso.

Our teller's hometown of Kumasi lies inland from the coast, about 250 kilometers from the capital, Accra. Kumasi, the second largest city in Ghana, had a 1984 population of 376,246. It is the center of a cocoa-producing region.[1] Since the 1700s, Kumasi has been the traditional seat of the Asante kings. At that time, the chief of Kumasi united several small states. The Golden Stool of the Asante was said to descend from heaven and rest on the knees of Osei Tutu, the first Ashantehene, who was guided by his priest Okomfo Ankye. This Golden Stool became the focal point for the creation of the Asante confederacy.[2]

Peter Pipim. Photo courtesy of Peter Pipim.

Meet Peter Pipim

Peter Pipim was born April 17, 1938, in Patase Kumasi, Ghana. He grew up there among his Asante people. The Asante (Ashanti) are members of the Akan language and culture group. Peter grew up in a tradition in which storytelling was a part of family life. Peter now lives in Washington, D.C., where he recently retired from his work as education specialist for the National Museum of African Art, an affiliate of the Smithsonian Institution. Beginning in 1977, when he began using storytelling for Kwanza programs, Peter incorporated storytelling and the sharing of information about storytelling traditions into his educational work at the museum. He was also a storytelling trainer for other museum workers.

Talking with Peter Pipim

In January 1992, Peter gave a workshop titled "Principles of African Storytelling" at the Seattle Art Museum. After the workshop, I interviewed Peter in his hotel room.

I asked Peter when he first heard stories.
    As far back as I can remember. As far back as being a child who is beginning to walk or whatever . . . stories are being told. Your mother laughs, you know, in the community circle. That's the way it begins.
    So you get up. You can walk. And so you walk yourself into the group that are telling the story. Then . . . you get to the point where you can tell stories also.

    It begins very early.
    You are carried there.
    And then you walk there.
    And then you . . . begin telling stories.
    So that's how it is.

I asked Peter if there were some storytellers he liked especially well as a child.
    In every community there are one or two individuals . . . when they are *there,* then you know it is going to be a *good* night session. Because they are good. It is an artistic thing. There are many individuals that . . . "Oh! John is there?" Maybe stop everything they are doing and come over because . . . those tellers *make* things go *right* . . . when they are there.

I think of this one woman, Nana Taadu, oooh, she was *good*. She was the wife of one my uncles. And this woman was good. She passed many years ago. And when she was in a storytelling session . . . I mean *hush!* (*Peter leaned forward with his hand cupped to his ear as if to catch every word of this teller.*) I mean you don't swivel your ears to anywhere, but to exactly . . . point to point of what she is saying. There are people who have that reputation. And she was extremely good.

I ask how it is decided who will tell next in a telling session.

The story has a formal beginning and a formal ending. You begin with a call and the audience responds, and you call back and begin the story. At the end, "If the story that I narrated, whether it is good or bad . . . let this one go and another one *come*."

So the next person calls and the audience responds.

You stay where you are. You will be sitting in circles so you can . . . maybe one tells one here . . . and the next one is on the other side . . . and the next one will be in the middle. The first to respond at the end of a story is the next teller.

Peter explains that the storytelling generally takes place outside in the court-yard.

Rooms are a private place. The courtyard is the common place. So [story-telling takes place] out in the courtyard, or even outside the house. The Asante architecture . . . it's rectangular. Depending on the size of the house, there might be four or five rooms on this side, three rooms on this side, five rooms on this side, and two rooms here. Then you have a courtyard, where activities are centered around. So rooms are the private places.

If folks from other courtyards *hear* . . . people are enjoying themselves . . . it invites people. It's *inside* [the courtyard] so they *hear* it, so they are com-ing. We wouldn't go out and announce . . . "Hey, come on, we're going to do storytelling." It's the *intensity* that will invite people.

Since storytelling takes place in the evening, after dark, a different set of aes-thetics governs the telling.

The difference between performance as an artist of the stage, as com-pared to the traditional storyteller performer, is that in the night, gestures cannot be seen. So the [vocal] emphasis in the stories is more significant. It takes more *tonal* expression . . . more tonal gesture. Not body language. On the stage, in the morning or in the day, you use body language to commu-nicate. But in the traditional setting when it is the night, body language cannot be read. All this has to be in the *tone* in which the story is narrated. And therefore some storytellers will make the same story *more* palatable and *more* entertaining . . . more *lively*. Depending on what kind of *tone* they use.

In his performance at the Seattle Art Museum, Peter had used songs interjected into stories. I asked if I had understood correctly that the song did not necessarily have to be used for a particular story.

There are no songs that are set aside for a story. Well, some stories come with their own songs. That, of course, is different. Because the song is part of that story. But the songs that are used within stories, as I was doing, are interchangeable. Within the story. There are lots of these. I can't give you a figure, but let's say there are many.

But it seems that in the village there are some of those songs that are more easily [used] in terms of call and response. And there are some of them that also capture the audience or the participants. Captures their imagination, so they *like* it. So you may hear the same song used over and over in *one* night. Because, maybe they *like* it.

Peter had demonstrated by using an assistant from the audience to interject the song into his story. I ask if there is an appropriate time to interject the song, and whether any audience member can initiate the singing interlude.

Yes, [anybody in the audience might start the song]. The appropriate time is when the teller has come to a . . . let's say a *stop*. And that's the appropriate time to stop the person and come interject the song. And then after the song, the teller begins again from where they stopped.

I noticed that the audience assistant had interjected the song right at the most exciting part. I ask if that is a good place to interject.

Exactly! She was very good. I think she was from a Baptist church. She was using that experience. And it worked precisely, because . . . when something is said which is exciting the story . . . you want to fill it up with a song. Or . . . if something exciting is going to happen . . . because you know the story . . . you want to *heighten* the excitement. So you come with a song. And then . . . the excitement *comes*.

Would the audience use this technique even in stories that had their own songs?

Yes. Stories are all songs. Songs, interchanging songs, clapping hands. That makes stories interesting. Because you don't sit there and just listen. You are *part* of it. So it is a communal participation.

Must the story be told in the same way every time?

It would be the same every time. That's why we have this counterbalance of . . . "Are you changing something in the story . . . which is known already?" If it's *known*. That you know the story and you are changing something . . . then of course you are going to make it known that you are not doing it right. If it is a new story which came from somewhere, let's say that one has traveled to another place. And came upon a story which is unknown here. Then they would take anything that is said.

Another is, if you would take a story . . . but someone tells you a story that they had from the original source . . . and *they* change things. Then it becomes questionable.

I wonder if someone could change the ending, or change girls to boys in the story.

No. No. No. No. He has to do it exactly the *way* it was said. But the tonal pattern will make the story his or her own. Like I said, the gesture comes from the tone. So the tonal aspect is very important. You can say in simple words, "I will go." Now . . . (*Peter demonstrates with dramatic tone*) "I would like to *go.*" You make it sound different. You can say the word a lot differently. But it is the same word. You don't change the context.

Peter explained that there are more than a dozen Akan peoples who share similarities in cultures and linguistics. The Asante are part of this group. The languages are close enough for stories to pass from one culture to another. He had been explaining that stories sometimes have to do with the locale in which they are told.

When you go to areas where they are going to live by the water, you have fishermen, and you have a whole lot of stories that deal with a body of water. And then when you go to the farming community, stories have to do more with farming. Stories have to do with hunters . . . if hunters are part of the session, you always come up with something about hunting in the story. So that is the nature of . . . but stories can also *travel.* Somebody might come from, let's say Mali. Come to Asante and settle, you know a farmer. He tells the story too. The story is a *Mandinka* story. Now it is told in Asante. Because somebody came, narrated the same story, and it picked up. So that is why I say stories travel too.

I asked Peter how he began telling stories in the United States.

I got into this storytelling maybe about 1977 or '78 because in the museum where I worked; it was a private museum, the Museum of African

Art. As a private institution, we used to do workshops on Kwanza celebrations. And that's where this storytelling started coming in, because every principle . . . Umoja . . . Kujichagulia . . . all these principles. On each day, we would think about a story that relates the principle of the day. So there were programs, and people come to the museum to listen to stories relating to those principles. That got me started. So from then on I used storytelling a lot.

Now storytelling became a part of my programming. I coordinate, as a matter of fact, the Smithsonian African art storytelling people at the National Museum of African Art.

After Peter's telling of the Ananse story (given below), I ask about the violence in the tale. "Would there be any complaint from parents about beating on the dwarf's hump?"

The moral of the story is that Ananse was greedy because he wanted to have more rain than his son. And so instead of using small sticks to play, he thought, the more he would hit this person, the more rain he would have. He did not think that hitting him hard would kill him. So that was the end, the result of it. If you are not greedy, you do things that remain humanly possible. Because of the greediness that's exactly what happened.

And again wasn't that part of the morals? When you have a friend that you trust, to what extent can we trust ourselves? Because Ant trusted Ananse like he was going to come back. Ananse was gone, never to be seen again. So he was carrying the coffin. So there is a limitation to things that we do. And we have to weigh them very carefully. See? Ananse violated that trust.

So . . . I have told the story in audiences that are mixed. And nobody sees anything wrong with the violence, because the violence that is happening is getting to a point. See the point supersedes the incidents that preceded it. Don't go too extreme. Don't go too far. So it tells you not to do it.

During the telling, Peter talked through his nose in a funny manner when speaking for Ananse. I ask about this.

Ananse is always . . . talking nose. That's a characteristic of Ananse.

The whole story among the Akan is centered around Ananse. That's why we call it *Anansesem* . . . Ananse stories.

Let me give you this story. I think I like this story very much. The name of this story is, "Why Ants Carry Bundles of Things That Are Bigger Than Themselves."

Peter's Story

WHY ANTS CARRY BUNDLES OF THINGS THAT ARE BIGGER THAN THEMSELVES

Once upon a time
Kwaku Ananse
the trickster
was when . . . as we all know . . . was married . . .
he had children . . .
his wife's name was Aso.
His older son was called Ntikuma.
When Ntikuma had grown to be a man
then he farmed side by side with his father.
So this is farming people.

Ananse . . . his farm . . . and his son . . . were very good farmers . . .
and they could produce a lot.
Of course he learned the art of farming from his father.
And he was as good as his father.

One day, one season . . . they planted . . . hoping it would rain as usual.
The rain would come down as it always does.
This time . . . the rain didn't come down as they expected.
One moon had gone by.
No rain.
Second moon had gone by.
There was no *rain*.
Well a farmer will get tired of planting . . . and no rain.
So the seeds are going to get rotten . . . in the soil.

Well one morning Ntikuma, Ananse's son, got up in the morning.
There hasn't been rain yet.
As concerned as he was . . . he walked to the farm.
To see what was going on there.
While he was going.
He saw a dwarf.
I mean right in front of him in the middle of nowhere.
The dwarf looked at this young man, Ntikuma.
"You look like you are very dejected.

Young man, what's wrong?"
The man said, "Well. You have seen it, right?
And you are right.
I am very disturbed.
Because since many moons ago . . .
I haven't seen a drop of rain."

He said, "Oooohh. That's why you are worried?"
He said, "Of course. Yes.
If I eat . . . what remains of my seedlings?
Then of course, I won't have anything left to plant."
Then the dwarf said, "Well Ntikuma. I may be able to help you.
If you go under the rules."
He said, "I will do anything you ask me. As long as I can do it."
He said, "Okay. (*very dignified*)
I am going to ask you to take me to your farm.
And you put me in the middle of your farm.
I mean right in the center of your farm.
And you give me a log to sit down in your farm.
Then I will ask you to go back to the bushes again
and cut yourself two small sticks.
And you come over . . . and you are going to play . . .
on my hunchback.
And as you play on my hunchback,
I will do the singing.
And I will vibrate the sky.
The rain is going to come down."

Well Ntikuma was so excited.
He took him . . . go out to the middle of the farm . . .
went to the corner and cut a wood and cut a piece of block
and brought it down . . . so he sat down.
Run back to the bushes again
and cut himself two small sticks and came back.
Said, "Okay.
You play upon my hunch.
And I will sing for you."
So he went on his hunch with this little stick.
"Kutuum ta
Kutuum ta . . ."

Well he was playing . . . good rhythms.
Then the dwarf was singing.
"Nsuot
Nsuot . . ."
Mean:
"Rain come down.
Rain pour.
We want you.
We want to see you."
So the dwarf was singing this.
"Rain *come* down.
Pour."
Well. It didn't take the dwarf long.
The skies opened up.
It *poured.*
It *poured.*
Until his farm . . . was *wet.*
It didn't rain anyplace . . . but Ntikuma's farm.
The young man was very happy.
He came home,
knowing very well that things were going well on his farm.
In a couple of days,
his father, Ananse,
decided to go . . . walk out to the farm.
(*talking through the nose for Ananse*)
He went there . . . and saw that his son's . . .
crops are growing . . .
and his are still in the ground!
How could this happen?
He was *shocked.*
How could this happen?
We are just side by side.
And Ananse ran home.
And by the time he got to the edge of the village,
he started yelling.
"Ntikuma . . . eee! Ntikuma . . . eee! Ntikuma . . . eee!" (*pronounced "aye"*)
The young man heard the father at a distance and *knew* what had happened.
The father has gone to the farm . . .

and saw the difference between his farm and *his* farm.
So . . . he stepped out of the house and said.
"Heyyyy. Daddy I'm *here*. I'm *here*." (*in whiny nasal tone*)
"Ntikuma. I went to the farm.
And I *saw* . . . your farm . . .
everything is growing up.
Mine are still *dead* . . . on the ground.
You going to tell me . . .
what *you* did to have rain in your farm
and I didn't have a drop of rain in *my* farm."

Well. The son knew his Daddy how he is.
He was first reluctant . . . very apprehensive to tell exactly what happened.
Because he knew his father.
What he would do.
Anyway. Your father is your father.
So.
He told his father the whole story . . . about going to the farm and
the dwarf coming right in the middle of things . . . asking why
he was worried . . . and he told him exactly . . . that he was worried
because there was no rain for many moons . . . and took him to
the middle of the farm . . . cut a log for him to set down . . .
cut some small sticks . . . and then of course he played music
on his back . . . and it rained.
So the father, Ananse, said,
(*in nasal tone, dropping voice off in whine at end of each line*)
"Is that all that *you* did?
And you had rain?
OK?
I am not going to wait . . .
to go to the bushes to cut the sticks tomorrow.
I'm going to the bush and cut my sticks right now . . .
and keep it in my room.
And I take it with me tomorrow . . .
and go beat him . . .
and get some rain too."
He went to the bushes and cut himself sticks . . .
as big as this, yeah? (*showing width of upper arms*)
Two of them.

Brought it home.
Put it in his room.
And went to sleep.

Next,
first cock crow
Ananse was up.
Sharping his knife . . . everything . . . getting ready to farm.
He was going to the farm . . . with the two sticks on his back.
Tied up to his body.
Hidden.
OK?

So.
The midget.
The dwarf.
Came by.
And stopped right in the middle of Ananse
and said, "Oh. Kwaku? What's wrong with you?
Did your wife divorce you?"
Said "Oh . . . no . . . no . . . no . . ."
"What . . . is any of your children sick?"
"No . . . no . . . no . . . no . . . no . . .
"We all were fine,
my wife she loves me.
Everybody, everything is fine.
But,
I planted many moons ago.
I haven't seen a drop of rain."
Then . . . the dwarf said,
"Ohhh. Is that why . . . your face looks so droopy?
Well I can help you.
If you will go by the rule.
Then I will *lay* down."
Ananse replied.
"I will do anything you ask me to do."
Then the dwarf said, "Well. Would you take me to your farm,
and sit me right in the middle of the farm?
Then you going to find me a log . . . to sit down.
Then you going to go back in the bushes to cut the sticks.

Then you going to play on my hunch.
Then *you* will have rain."

Ananse was so impatient he couldn't take this out to the middle of the
    row.
He just jumped into the farm and said,
"Right here! Let's do it right here."
The dwarf said, "Okay.
You get me the sticks,
the block to sit on,
and I will give you the rain."
So Ananse went to the corner and brought the log.
So the dwarf sat down.
And the dwarf says to Ananse,
"Would you go back and cut two small sticks
and play the music on my hunch?"
Ananse says, "Oh . . . no, no, no, no . . .
You don't have to worry about that.
I brought my own sticks already."
He went in back
and took his two large sticks.
And went on this guy.
On his back.
And he was hitting him.
(*exclamations!*)
He was hitting so good.
He was hitting and hitting and hitting.
He hit him so hard that the dwarf fell down . . . dead.

Whooo!
Ananse committing a murder?
How possible? Somebody did it.
Not Ananse.
So Ananse took this dead body.
Put it on the shoulder.
On the corner of the farm . . . there was a big old cola nut tree there.
Climbed the tree.
Put the midget on two branches.
Came down.
Ananse came down and sat down,

not too far from the cola nut tree,
and sat there.
Cola is the nut of the . . . open and chew it . . . it's a stimulant.
So people come by.
And if there's none on the ground,
they climb up and get some.
So he knew somebody was going to come and get cola.
And that person would be the person who killed the midget.
So he sat there.
And he sat.
He sat.
He sat.
He sat.
The sun was going down.

Well. His son . . . was worried.
Daddy has been on the farm . . . since morning.
The sun is going . . .
he usually comes home early,
but today . . . the sun is going down . . .
and he's not home.
So as a concerned son,
he was going to see what had happened to the father.

He went to the farm.
Saw his father sitting under a tree
not too far from the cola nut tree.
So he said, "Daddy? Did you find the dwarf?"
He said, "I find him all right.
He went in the cola nut tree to get some cola.
And I been sitting here since morning.
He hasn't come down yet."
Then his son said, "Daddy. Don't worry.
He knows me better.
Let me go get him.
And maybe he can help you."
The young man climbed up the cola tree.
He put his hand on the dwarf.
The dwarf fell.
Dead.

Ananse jumped up from the tree that he was sitting on.
"You my son!
How could you do that?
You have killed the dwarf!
He is very respected in the community.
And you killed him?
My son . . . You are in trouble!"

"Innocent . . . murder . . . is punishable.
You know that?"
The son said,
"Yes, Daddy.
I know.
But.
When I was coming to get you . . .
the king . . .
announced to the whole town . . .
that anybody who . . .
would bring this midget . . .
dead or alive . . .
would get a reward."
Ananse said,
"What did you *say*?"
And he said, "The king wants this midget, dead or alive for a reward.
So.
I'm going to take him and get my reward."
The daddy said,
"Oh, no, no, no, no . . .
Son, you didn't do *anything*.
I'm going to take him.
And go to the king
and get my reward.
Because I did it."
So the son said, "Yes.
If you want to get your reward yourself.
Then *you* do it."
So Ananse took this . . . corpse on his shoulder.
Walked straight home.
To the king's palace.
Dropped the dead body in front of the king,

who was sitting with his councillors . . . discussing.
So he asked him, "What are you doing?"
He said "I *killed* him.
And I want my reward."
He said, "You *killed* a human being?
And you want me to reward you?"
Ananse was *tried* on the spot.
And he was condemned that the punishment
he was going to get was death.

A coffin will be built.
And the dwarf will be put in that coffin.
And Ananse will carry that coffin
as long as he lives.
That coffin could not be set down.
He had to carry it.
That was the curse
of the state . . . of the chief . . .
on Ananse.
He will carry the coffin
sleeping
working
eating
doing everything.

Ananse carried this curse . . . for a long while.
Nobody would help Ananse . . .
because it's not supposed to touch the ground.
So if anybody's going to help you,
that person is going to have to carry it so that he could have rest.
Well one day Ananse met Ant.
He said, "Ant, (*nasal tone*)
I need to go to the market.
To buy a couple of things.
And I cannot carry this with *me* to the market.
Could you help me . . . and I will be right back . . .
and get it."
Ant said, "Don't we know you.
Ha.
You want somebody to carry your thing for you and you are *gone*.

You are going to trick me into it."
"Unh-hunh," he said.
"No, no, no, no.
I won't do that, my good friend, to you.
You are my good friend.
I won't do that to you.
I will come back and get it."
Ant trusted Ananse.
Took the coffin.
Put it on his head.
Ananse went to the market not to be seen again.
He didn't *come* back.

Ant has been carrying that coffin ever since.
And that's why we see ants . . . they are carrying bundles of things.
We don't even *see* them but we see the objects are *moving*.

It's because of them.
And that is the way it is.

Notes

1. Statistics from http://www.cia.gov/cia/publications/factbook/geos/ and from www.ghanaweb.com/GhanaHomePage/geography/kumasi.php.

2. For photographs of contemporary Kumasi, see http://www.galenfrysinger.com/kumasi.htm.

Peter's Bibliography

Peter tells me that his papers are all in Ghana now, and Peter is in Washington, D.C. He was unable to provide a bibliography of his articles, and I was unable to discover any in my searches.

Curtis DuPuis. Photo courtesy of Curtis DuPuis.

10

Curtis DuPuis
A Family Tradition

*Stories are just one fragment of my knowledge that
I remember.*
CURTIS DUPUIS

BACKGROUND INFORMATION ABOUT THE CHEHALIS

Our teller's people, the Chehalis, reside mostly in and around the
4,224.63-acre Chehalis Reservation in southwestern Washington state.
The reservation was established in 1860 for the Upper Chehalis and
Lower Chehalis peoples. The Chehalis had not signed a treaty with the
government but had homesteaded their lands. In 1866, 3,753.63 acres
were given for homestead entry to the Chehalis, and 471 acres were set
aside for schools. The tribe, however, had decreased from an estimated
5,000 in 1855 to 149 by 1906. Diseases and alcohol-related deaths had
taken a terrible toll on the people. The 2000 census showed 388 Native
Americans living on the Chehalis Reservation.

The Lower Chehalis were a seaside people relying on fish and shellfish for trade. The Upper Chehalis were a riverine people, supplement-
ing fish with roots and berries from the plains and mountains and
traveling by horseback far into the interior to trade.

A statement from the Confederated Tribes of the Chehalis notes the
closeness these people feel to their ancestors:

In the old days we gathered sacred roots and berries. We fished the Chehalis, Black, Cowlitz, Satasop, Wynoochee, Elk, Johns, Skookumchuck, and Newaukum rivers. Our people fished and hunted from the mountains, across the prairie, to Grays Harbor and in the lower Puget Sound.

In the old days the baskets carried and stored our foods. We relied upon the baskets, the rivers, the land, the roots, the berries, the fish, and the animals. Our lives were tied together by the Creator.

Today we live on a reservation between the Black and Chehalis rivers near Oakville. We operate a Tribal Government, a convenience store, a health clinic, a housing authority, The Lucky Eagle Casino, an early childhood development center, youth computer training center, and several other programs. Our major focus is to become a self sufficient organization.

Today we live the contemporary life, but our hearts still travel where our ancestors lived and died.[1]

Meet Curtis DuPuis

Curtis DuPuis lives near the Chehalis Reservation in southwestern Washington state. Raised on the reservation and trained in many cultural traditions by his elders, Curtis now tries to pass this information on to the younger generation. He is a trained management consultant and works with the state government in Olympia managing contracts. But Curtis makes time to come, when asked, to share stories and traditions of his people. I first met Curtis in 1985 when a mutual friend, Sally Porter, brought him to the Bothell Library to tell stories to our children. Curtis told stories, sang, and led the children in a charming rabbit dance. In 1987 I invited Curtis to speak at a retreat in which traditional tellers were able to share in a living room environment with small groups of teachers, librarians, and storytellers. The tapes from his three sessions, plus tapes from a National Association for the Preservation and Perpetuation of Storytelling conference in 1993, provide the basis for his words and stories here.

Curtis Speaks of His Traditions

Curtis Introduces His People

My name is Curtis Levi DuPuis.[2]

And I belong to the Hazel Pete family of the Chehalis Reservation, Oakville, Washington.

All in all it is not that I just know stories . . . but that I know all these other activities . . . and stories are just one fragment of my knowledge that I remember.

I am a young man, I am forty-three years old. I was born in 1944 and I lived on the reservation until I left home in 1962. We had thirty-seven houses on the reservation. We all owned our lots. Eighty acres or seventy acres. So the houses were far apart. You'd go another eighth of a mile or another quarter of a mile and you would come to the next house. And so we were all relatives. There were five major families and three minor families. I belonged I guess to one of the minor families. There were about eighty or ninety people in our family . . . our lineage.

For the Chehalis, we always say that we lived there since time began. We were one of the few Indian tribes which never had to relocate, when the white man arrived.

Curtis explains that the Chehalis signed a treaty that was never ratified, and they refused to sign again. Thus, they were never moved from their own land.

In 1867 the white men, they came by. And they talked to the Chehalis. They said, "We can go to Olympia. This year. If everyone has five dollars, then you can get 160 acres of land. They said, you should go with us." We said, "What does five dollars look like?" And they said three fish, or five skins, or ten pounds of berries or something. So we said, "We'll go with you." So the Indians and the white men went up to Olympia and we homesteaded our reservation. So we ended up with 4,440 acres . . . And that's where we'd always lived.

Learning the Geographic Places of the Land

The other thing that helped me learn all these things . . .

When I was thirteen and older I'd get in the pickup and I'd drive my grandma and grandpa to go and get things for their baskets and to visit people.

They'd say, "Go this way."

They'd say, "That's where we camped when we were going to the mountains."

"That's where we camped when we shot the deer."

"That's where we camped and we caught the fish."

They'd say, "Turn here. That's where we got the baskets."

Fifty years ago.

And so I was lucky, being in the car at that time . . . listening to these people talk.

And we'd go around this mountain and she'd say,

"That's where we went to get roots . . . or get berries . . ."

So here I am sixteen years old, driving this pickup.

And Grandma and Grandpa are reciting the geographic areas of the place.

So I was lucky in having that type of background.

That's how I learned what I know today.

The opportunity of telling a story . . . is to know a story.

And to *know* a story means you already have similar experiences.

You just have to say them, that's all.

Maybe what you think is goofy, *is* a story.

If you say it once . . . you say it twice . . . maybe it *is* a story after all.

And if you say it and no one understands it, maybe you didn't say it clear enough.

Or maybe the audience wasn't right after all.

Preserving Memories

You can go ahead and have these memories.

These things which allow me to go backwards.

I think that when you talk to old people . . .

When I talk to my aunt who is eighty-four now,

Or when I talk to older tribal members,

Or when I talk to my mom . . .

I think that you can go into a trance.

And they begin to recite.

You can begin to remember when you were a younger person.

And a lot of times you can remember the conversations you had,

like when my uncle Morris Penn was there.

And my mom would say, "Remember when Morris Penn was here,

he was sitting over there.

And we were talking about going to the ocean."

And she would start reciting something.

If you pause enough,
and you become relaxed,
and you really strive for these moments,
that you can go back to a conversation twenty or thirty years ago
and you can remember the inflections that people had.

And I think this is a talent which everyone could use . . . or has . . .
And could nourish and develop.
But you have to remember that my background is different.
I have an interest in doing this, compared to someone else who was told,
"Oh I wish you'd be quiet. I'm missing out on my show." Or . . .
"Quiet now . . . here's the rerun."

For those of us who take the time to understand and to develop the memory.

Curtis is upset sometimes with his own twin thirteen-year-old daughters. He wants to take them gathering, and they prefer to sit home and watch TV shows. He says they have already seen them six times before.
   I want to take a few minutes and go get some berries.
   Or go back and get the basket material . . .
   It's only a symbolic gathering.
   We know that we need the basket material.
   And we know we can go to a new place and get our cattails.
   But sometimes I like to drive over this way twenty minutes to get to an old site.
   I say, "You know, when I was young . . . your size . . . this is where we were. And this is where Grandma said that *she* was."
   They don't see sometimes the value.

But I think that in my own effort at letting these relatives and nieces and nephews remember . . .
   that by showing them how many opportunities there were and there are . . .
   And how many of these people of our family that remember . . .
   That they will develop their appreciation and their memories too.
   So all of our material, except for today, is oral history.

Passing on the Traditions

Curtis clearly sees himself as merely a custodian of the culture. When asked if his brothers and sisters knew all these stories he knows, Curtis said of course they did. When asked if they told them, he avoided answering, explaining that each person in the group develops special skills to share with the others. When asked who had made his deer-rattle staff, he said, "Everybody did." Then he explained about their cultural days for the children.

We have one day each month for what we call the seventh-generation children. We have a cultural day for them. We start early in the morning. During the material-gathering time we will go to the beach and get grass, or we'll go to the river and get more grass. And we'll show them how to do that. How to separate it and sort it.

In the winter when things are wet, we will show them how to make designs, or how to choose their colors, and what the different colors mean.

We'll let them practice making different things. And then in the evening we'll take them to a movie or go and get pizza or something like that.

We try to let them know that our family is a very extended family and we have a lot of cultural knowledge. And if they take the time they can learn too.

If you keep your ears open and you watch, you are going to see a lot of things.

There are a lot of nuances to culture.

A lot of different colors,

a lot of different fabrics,

a lot of different materials.

And they can see that they have the world's best teachers.

It is hard to beat the quality of our family's handicrafts.

Bedtime Stories

Curtis tells about playing around from house to house with his cousins when he was a child and about the elders walking from house to house to visit.

When we were young then . . .

Around seven or eight o'clock . . .

Because we didn't have electricity.

We'd be getting ready for bed.

And for all the little kids they would say . . .

"If you people would lay down . . .
we'll tell you a story."

And many times the stories were the stories of the family.
And I didn't realize this.
Because I didn't know that the things I speak about today, were innate.
They were a part of my being.

Stories are for the family.
Most of our stories are for the family.
They are not for the tribe and they are not for outsiders.
They are for the family.
So when we are together, we are having supper, a birthday, Christmas or something.
We would finally come to that time in the celebration that we would say, "We would want someone to tell a few stories."
This would be a time to go through the lineages and recite who our relatives were, where the houses are . . . things like that. And we would go ahead and tell a few stories.

So someone would make the introductions.
We would all know each other anyway because we are all relatives.
But there are some formalities to observe.
It just wasn't stand up and say "Little Red Riding Hood."
And we would take the time to make a good introduction.

We would basically tell just one story, for one occasion.
So it would take you twenty or thirty parties to hear everything.
And you might hear the same story twice in a row, depending on the audience.
But there would have to be a formal introduction.
"We are glad that you're here today . . . and we hope you enjoyed eating your turkey . . . and one of the things we want to do is listen to a story from our aunt here . . . who just came in from . . ." Things like that.

Only after giving his lineage, introducing his people, will Curtis tell a story. He brings along a fascinating array of costumes that his family have made by hand and explains each piece as he puts it on. Then he lifts his deer-rattle story-telling staff and is ready to tell. For the chanting in some stories he uses a small square drum. Curtis has a sizable repertoire of tales. During the sessions, which lasted three and a half hours, at the Traditional Tellers Retreat, he told six different tales. Two of Curtis's stories appear below.[3]

Curtis's Stories

MOSQUITOES

Curtis always introduces his stories with chat, then launches directly into the tale.

When we tell the stories . . . they aren't just recited like story number one and story number two. It would have been more likely one day, someone would tell this story. And then maybe at nighttime, another person would tell another story. And you wouldn't have told . . . many stories just in one afternoon. It would not have been our function to do that.

The other thing is . . . when we tell our stories . . . if I were to be the storyteller . . . or my mom were to be the storyteller . . . we would have had an introduction. A formal presentation . . . a realization . . . that something important was going to happen. Everyone is talking. But at a time when this is going to be one of the main events of the program or the remembrance . . . there would be a definite introduction . . . a formal introduction . . .

The person would say . . . "I want to tell you the story about a long time ago."

So you go . . . (*pounds story stick three times*)

You get their attention and then you want to tell the story about . . . "Did you hear 'Mosquitoes'? Want to hear that one?"

A long time ago, when the earth was young,
and people and animals lived together,
there was this village . . . on the Chehalis.
This village down there where all the animals . . . like elk . . . mouse . . . fox . . . people . . .
they all lived in the village.
In those days you could all talk back and forth so that everyone could understand each other.
And also in this village there was one family that was called "mosquitoes."
In those days mosquitoes were a lot different from what they are today.

In those days the adult mosquitoes were maybe about the size of a soccer ball.

You know . . . large.

And the teenagers were about the size of a hardball or a softball.

Then all the infants . . . all the babies . . . are the ones that are here today.

You know . . . those little tiny ones.

Anyway, what happened was that all these mosquitoes would come by and they would bite you.

And because they were much larger, when they bit you they would take a lot of meat and suck out a lot of blood.

So you would be sick. And you'd have to go home.

And you'd have to rest until you got well.

So anyway, all these people and animals got together.

And they were here, and they said, "Well we should do something about those mosquitoes. We should teach them a lesson."

Finally one said, "Why don't we go ahead. Why don't we have a *big* supper.

Let's cook something that those mosquitoes will eat.

And invite them to be the guests of honor.

And when they are . . . they'll eat.

And when they get done eating they'll be big and fat.

They won't be able to fly too high,

and they won't be able to fly too fast.

We'll hit 'em over the head. We'll throw them into the fire."

And they said, "That sounds like a good idea.

That's what we want to do."

So . . . "When you go home tonight . . .

Every time you see a mosquito . . . say, 'Come to supper tomorrow night.

You're the guest of honor. We want you to eat first.'"

And all the animals said, "That's a good idea."

So they did.

So they started walkin' home . . . at noon time . . . at two o'clock . . .

They'd see these mosquitoes.

"Tomorrow night . . . we're going to this place we call Boho. (*Bull Hole, pronounced bo-ho*)

You're the guest of honor.
And you get to eat first.
It'll be at suppertime."

All the mosquitoes were really excited.
This was the first time it had ever happened to them.

"We're glad of this honor.
We appreciate this."

So the next day came . . .
And these people and animals went to Boho.
They got there about noon.

They had three great big pots.
And they started making bean stew.
They cooked and they cooked and they cooked.

It was suppertime; it started getting dark.
And all the soup was ready.
And all the people and animals were waiting there.

Well, like I told you . . . these mosquitoes were big.
And they started coming in.
They had to set on the trees.
Mosquitoes today they always hide in the brush and on the grass and
everything?
Well, in those days the mosquitoes were big and had to lay in those trees.
Well, those limbs were . . . almost ready to break . . . because there were so
many mosquitoes.

Finally one of them says, "Hey! What did you cook? What's for supper
tonight?"
Because they couldn't see what was in the pot.

One of the animals says, "Bean soup! Bean soup!
Come on! You're the guest of honor. You can eat first!"

Those mosquitoes up in the trees said, "Aw, my goodness, we don't eat
bean soup.

We're sorry, but we can't eat supper with you tonight.
We don't eat bean soup.
Maybe you can invite us another time."

And the animals said, "That's all right.
We're sorry. But maybe another time we can do this."

So the mosquitoes went home.

The people and animals ate up all this bean soup . . . it was very good soup.
And they said, "We should try it again.
Let's go down to a place we call Skookumchuck.
We'll be down there and . . . we'll do it again . . . tomorrow night.
So tomorrow . . . every time we see a mosquito . . . we'll tell them we're going to Skookumchuck and we want 'em to eat. 'You'll be our guests of honor.'"

So they said, "That's good."

So . . . they invited those mosquitoes again.
They got there about noon at Skookumchuck.
And this time they made fish soup.
Three great big pots.
They had fish, and onions, and carrots, potatoes, and rice and everything.
Real good soup.

At suppertime all those mosquitoes were there and they said,
"What did you cook for supper tonight?
What is that over there?
I don't understand that smell. What is that?"

The people and animals said, "Fish soup!
Come on now . . . you're the guest of honor!
Come eat first! You can eat first."

The mosquitoes said, "Oh, my goodness, we don't eat fish soup. We'll have to go home."

So the people and animals ate it up.
They said, "Well what are we going to do?"
They said, "Well . . . we'll go down to Black River."
They said, "This time . . . we really have to be there at noon.
And we're going to make this soup.
And everyone has to be there."

Well, the next day everyone was there at noon.

This wise man said, "Make two lines! Everyone in line!
Make two lines!
We're going to make this soup."

So here's all these people.
They all started getting in line.
Everyone was trying to look around to see what they were doing.
"What are they doing?"
"How come we are in line here?"
"What type of soup is this?"
They were all excited.

Finally the man says, "All right, Elk, you're first. Come here."
So Elk comes up to these three big pots.
He says, "Give me your hoof."
Elk gives him a hoof.
And he has this knife.
He cuts the hoof and some blood drips out.
He says, "Next!"
And it was a bird.
He got some blood.
"All right . . . you over there . . . come here!"
He got some more blood.

Finally it was Bear's turn.
"Come on Bear!
Give me a paw!"

Bear says, "I'll give you a paw." (*threatening tone*)

"All right, Bear.

You can rest over there.
We'll get you next time."

They kept running through all the animals.
And here came Skunk.
"Give me your paw!"

Skunk says, "I'll give you my tail."
And he says . . . "You go rest with Bear."

Finally the three pots were full.
They were just full of blood.

They said, "Put 'em on the fire.
Let's start cooking."
Boy that old blood started boiling . . .
And they were watching . . .

Anyway, it was suppertime and all those mosquitoes were watching in all
those trees.
They said, "All right. What did you cook for supper tonight?
What is that?
It really smells delicious!"

They said, "Blood soup."

Those mosquitoes said, "Oh, my goodness. Blood soup. Did you hear
that?"
They said, "No one's ever done this before."
They got ready to eat.
They were really pleased.

There was just a great big maze of mosquitoes . . . big ones . . . little
ones . . . bigger ones.
They were buzzing around and they were eating.
Finally all the soup was gone.

They said, "Boy. We'll have to do this more often.
No one's ever done that before."
They said . . . "We'll have to go home now. It's getting dark."

Well, those mosquitoes tried to fly high.
And they couldn't get very high.
They said, "That's okay.
We'll just go along the trail with you people.
We'll just go that way."

And they started going.
But they couldn't go very fast, either.

All the people and animals were alongside of them.
And they were watching.

Finally one of the animals says, "All right, let's get 'em!
Hit 'em over the head and let's throw 'em in the fire."

Well, Elk and Deer have antlers. And they were sitting side by side, so they
said, "Let's charge."
So they ran through that big flock of mosquitoes with their antlers.
They got through . . . they had all these mosquitoes on their antlers.
So they pulled them off and threw them in the fire.

Over here on this side, Beaver was fighting.
He had got on a log.
He had his tail up.
Every time a mosquito would go by . . . (*slaps table hard*),
he'd hit it over the head with his tail.
And throw it in the fire.

Over here on this side, Skunk was fighting all by himself.
No one would help Skunk.
He had to kill his own mosquito and throw it in the fire.

Bear and Racoon, they had their claws.
People had their spears and sticks.

Finally the battle was over.
The only mosquitoes left were the little tiny ones.
And one of the animals says,
"Leave 'em alone.
We'll get 'em next time."

Curtis is silent until the audience realizes this is the end of the story. They laugh then and applaud. On reading this through, Curtis noted that "Indians generally wouldn't clap; they would raise both hands, shake three times, and rest their hands. No noise."

COYOTE AND THE FIELD MICE

After talking about his family background, the Hazel Pete family, and after showing some of the family-made artifacts he has brought along, Curtis picks up his story stick, hung with deer hooves. He asks his audience to guess what the deer hooves are. Then he explains that his family buys deer feet from other tribal members for fifty cents a foot. When they get enough, they boil them until the hoofs can be peeled off with pliers. Then you drill a hole in them and put designs on them. Curtis always prefaces a story with introductory chat.

The other thing that I have then is my talking stick. This is a straight piece of wood from vine maple. (*pounds stick and deer rattle loudly*) This is carved here with a bear with a fish in its mouth.

A long time ago you would see these. The talking stick would be about maybe eight inches wide and about thirty inches long, and probably weigh forty pounds. And here would be some old men. (*shakes rattles*) You had to use two hands to move them because they were so big. They'd use them for church, they'd use them for music, they'd use them for singing. And they'd go like that too. (*shakes rattles really hard*) So . . . I said I'm still young today. But maybe tomorrow I'll be old and I wanna be able to move my stick. When I'm old I wanna be able to move this. I don't wanna just have to go like that, you know. (*pounds stick slowly*)

So. This first story I want to tell you is . . . ever heard about Coyote before? What does a coyote sing? You know what a coyote is? (*audience affirms*) You don't know the story about Coyote. (*audience has heard some stories about coyotes*) How about you? Do you know how a coyote sings? (*audience member indicates "no"*)

Well, let me tell you a story about Coyote.

Curtis now shifts into a storytelling voice.
    A long time ago,
    when the earth was young,
    and people and animals lived together,
    there was this village . . . down on the Chehalis.

And the animals might have been bear, mouse, and people.

In those days you could talk back and forth so you could understand each other.

Anyway . . .
Early in the morning,
Like when you wanted to get up to go to the conference [Curtis had gotten up early to drive up from Chehalis to the conference],
All the coyotes in the family would get together.
They'd get on top of the hill.
And they'd sing a song.

Then you knew when it was time for lunch.
Because just before it was time to eat,
the coyotes would get together and go up on top of the hill
and sing another song.

And the thing that made most people mad was that
just when your kids were about asleep,
the coyotes would sing *another* song.

And this song that they sung was (*shakes rattle stick as intro and pounds as he chants*)
"Whoo! Whoo-whoo-WHOO! Whoo-Whoooooo!" (*last "Whoooooo" trails off down-scale*)
And they'd sing that song early in the morning,
at lunchtime, and at suppertime.

What that song meant was,
"Who has pretty long hair like me.
Who has pretty braids like us."

And they were very pleased and they'd sing that song.

Well, one night all of those coyotes were on top of the hill.
When they were done singing, they said,
"Well it's dark, it's sleep time, it's time to go home."
So they left. All except one.
One coyote was still there.

He thought he had the most pretty hair and the best braids.
He said, "I'll sing my song again."

Well, he was on top of that hill and he got ready to sing.
But just before he started, he heard some music.

"O-i-ho-WHEH-oh-ho. WHEH-oh-hooo." (*pounds deer-rattle stick in regular beat as intro and throughout chant*)

So Coyote was on top of that hill and he says,
"Oh my goodness, there's a party up here!"
He says, "I'm in luck tonight."
He says, "If I can find that party I'll have a *good* time."

Well, what I want to show you before I continue with this story is how animals hear better in the woods. What happens in . . . when animals are in the woods and they hear people walking about . . . breaking leaves, or walking on sticks, or walking on rocks, putting their shell in their gun ready to shoot them. When they hear that sound, usually they will stop and they'll look to see what it is that they heard . . . well, they will usually take their ears and make them flat. So if you will take your hands like this . . . make them flat and put them right next to your ears . . . you should be able to hear me speak a lot clearer.
So if I say, "One . . . two . . . three . . . four . . ." you should have heard that a lot better.

Well . . . when animals are in the woods . . .
Well, they'll stop . . . and they'll look like this . . .
and they'll say, "Oh. There's two people over there."
Or "Gee. They put a bullet in their gun."
And that's how they hear.

Well anyway . . .
Coyote was on top of that hill.
And he heard that music.
"Ooo-yo-ho-wheh . . . yo-ho-ho."

He put those ears up.
And he started walking around.

He was wondering where the party was.
He got closer and closer . . .
The music got louder and louder.
"Ooo-yo-ho-wheh . . . yo-ho-ho."

He found a little teepee here. A small one.
He said, "I'm lucky. I found a party.
I wonder who it is."

He reached down like that . . . and he looked inside the teepee.
He says, "OH! . . . Heavens! The field mice! My cousins.
I'm glad that I found you!
I'm glad that I'm here.
I'm ready to have a good time."

All those little field mice were looking like this . . .
They were looking up, they said, "Oh rats. It's Coyote."

They said, "Well. We're glad to see you, cousin.
We haven't seen you in a long time."

Coyote says, "Well, I'm sorry that I missed your invitation.
But I am here anyway.
You're lucky."

They said, "Yes, Coyote, we are lucky.
Lucky us."

They said, "This is a real fast party.
We didn't have time to let everybody know.
That's how come you weren't invited.
We forgot."

Coyote said, "That's okay."
I'm here. And I'm gonna have a good time.
And look! Right over there in the corner there's some rope.
Let me make myself small and I'm gonna sit over there."

They said, "Come on in, Coyote.
You can make yourself small and you'll be able to sit over here.

But you won't be able to stay all night,
because we don't have enough food or drink.

Coyote says, "Well, I don't eat very much.
I'm not very hungry.
And I hope you sing some songs."

So before they got ready to start again they gave Coyote some sandwiches.
He took about four.
They said, "Well, here's some munchies."
They had some oatmeal cookies.
He ate those too.

He said, "How about some juice?"

They just had a small cup, because mice are small.
He had about five cups.

They were worried because they were going to start running out of food.

Anyway, Coyote says, "Well I feel good now. Let's get ready to party!
I'll sing the first song.
You guys can help me out."

All those little field mice were here, they said,
"Aww . . . we already heard that song before Coyote.
We wanna sing different music.
You'll just have to be quiet and follow us.

Coyote says, "Okay. I'll do that."

They had a good party.
They stayed there all night.

It was morning time.

Coyote says, "Well, I'm tired.
I think I'll lay down right here. And I'll go to sleep.
I can't stay awake to walk home."
The field mice said, "It's alright, Coyote, lay down and go to sleep."

All those field mice were in there. About twenty-five of them.
They said, "How many sandwiches are left?"
They went to the basket and they looked.
It was empty.
They said, "Well, how many munchies are left?"
No. The munchies were gone.
They said, "Well, how about the juice?"
And it was empty also.
"What are we gonna eat for breakfast this morning?
What are we gonna eat?"

All those field mice were sittin' there and everything, they said,
"Well, what can we eat?" They were looking around and everything . . .
Finally one mouse looked at Coyote.
And everyone else looked at the ground.
And the second mouse looked at Coyote.
Finally all the mice were looking at Coyote.
They were looking there and finally one of them nodded their head.
Pretty quick all of the field mice were nodding their heads.

They went over there and they went to Coyote.
They took their knife.
And they cut off his braids.
Cut off his hair.
They took all those braids and they divided them up into equal pieces for everybody.
So they had breakfast.

They said, "When Coyote wakes up . . . he'll be mad."
The field mice decided they could not go back to their houses in the village.
Coyote would find the mice and hurt them.
"We'd better go in the woods.
We'll all have to go to a different house and hide.
We don't want Coyote to catch us, because he might eat us."
They said, "Who wants to live in the grass?"
Three or four of those mice raised their hands.
They said, "We'll live in the grass."

"Well, who wants to live in the blackberry vines and live in the brush?"
A couple more mice raised their hands. "That's where we'll live."

And how many more hiding places we got?
Someone said, "Let me hide in the woodshed.
I'll hide in the big pile of wood."

They said, "You can hide over there."

Finally they said, "Well what about you? You two over there?"

"We'd like living in a house.
I think we'll just go back home."

That's how come they live in a house with people.
Everyone had a place to hide.

They said, "We have to leave now.
Just to make sure we got time to get away, we should put something on
Coyote's head and tie it up. So that he won't catch us when he wakes up.
'Cause he'll be mad."

They went over there, and they got a mask.
They tied it on Coyote's head like this.

All the mice left to their new hiding places.

It was about noontime when Coyote woke up.
"Help me! Help me!
What is this on my head!
Help me! Help me!
I can't get it off!"
He couldn't get it off.

He said, "That's okay, I know the way home."
So he started walking.
But he couldn't see.
So he comes to all those places, you know, where the real sharp rock hurt
your feet.

"Ouch! Ouch!"
They really hurt his feet.

He walked this way and he fell off a cliff and hurt his head.
He walked over there and he bumped a log and he hurt his leg.
He went through the nettles. He went through the blackberry patch.
He finally got on top of the hill near his village.
But he was saying bad words.

All the people and animals were setting there in the village, watching and
waiting.

"What is that coming? Who is that?
It looks like a stranger! Who is that?"

Coyote got in the middle of the village.
"Help me! Help me!
Get this thing off my head!"
Help me! Help me!"

All the people around were just watching him.
"Is that a stranger? Or is it someone from our place?
Who is that?"

Finally a little elk boy was here, and he said,
"That might be Coyote in it."

Said, "We'll let's take that thing off of his head."
They took it off.

Coyote was there.

He said, "BOY. I really had a good party last night with those field mice.
But something was on my head and I couldn't see.
Now I get here and guys wouldn't help me.
But I'm glad that I'm home."

All these people and animals were sittin' around looking at Coyote.
They said, "What's the matter with you, Coyote?
How come you look funny?"

"I don't look funny. I'm the same old Coyote."
"Yeah, but something's different here, Coyote.
What happened to you?"

"I'm the same old Coyote."

Finally little Elk Boy says, "What happened to your hair, Coyote?
What happened to your hair?"

Coyote goes like this (*reaches with his hands for his braids*) and all of his braids are gone.
He goes like that and there is no more long hair.
He felt shamed and he felt bad.
He ran off and hid in the woods.

(*begins shaking talking stick rattles*)
So now when you hear him singing that song
"Woo-wo-wooooo. Woo . . . woo . . . woooooo . . ." (*imitating a coyote's call*)
He's saying, "Who took my braids?
What happened to my long pretty hair?"

Notes

1. Confederated Tribes of the Chehalis, http://www.chehalistribe.org/services.htm.
2. Taped in the living room of the officer's quarters at Fort Worden State Park, fall 1987. About twenty-five listeners, teachers, and storytellers who had come to hear traditional tellers for the weekend. Three tapes in possession of author. Also taped conference program at NAPPS Annual Conference, Seattle 1993. Two tapes in possession of author.
3. Traditional Tellers Retreat, Fort Worden State Park, fall 1987. Audience of twenty-five teachers and storytellers in living room setting. "Mosquitoes" was performed twice the same day to different groups. The tale varied in minor details from telling to telling, with improvisation around the tale plot. Curtis told "Coyote and the Field Mice" three times, in each of three sessions.

Curtis's Bibliography

Curtis has been asked by various publishers to put his stories into print. For complicated reasons involving family ownership of these stories, Curtis has not done this. It is a great honor that he has allowed some of his family stories to be reproduced here for scholarly use. Curtis gives permission for the oral sharing of his stories, but these tellings should be prefaced with the information that these are stories of the Hazel Pete family, as told by Curtis DuPuis.

Audio of Curtis in interview with Jens Lund is held at the Evergreen State College, http://www.evergreen.edu/library/ARCHWWW/FOLKLIFE/ FLCAudio.htm.

For information about the Governer's Heritage Award given to Hazel Pete, mother of Curtis, see http://www.arts.wa.gov/progFA/heritageAwd/2001 _pete.htm.

For information about Hazel Pete's work, see the Burke Museum website, http://www.washington.edu/burkemuseum/baskets/artists/snwc1 .html.

Hazel Pete's obituary with much of her bio appears in the online newsletter *Canku Ota* 78 (January 11, 2003), http://www.turtletrack.org/Issues03/ Co01112003/CO_01112003_Hazel.

11

Why Do They Tell?

We have seen that our tellers have many motivations for carrying on the social identity of storyteller. Robert J. Adams outlined several qualities necessary for creation of a master teller during his research with the Japanese elder teller Mrs. Tsune Watanabe. Roberts suggests that for a master teller to emerge, the following need be in place:

Teller hears tales, usually as a child.

Teller assumes the role of active teller.

Teller adopts tales as a means of personal expression and a validation of the teller's own attitudes.

Teller develops storytelling skills.

Teller connects with the audience.

Teller learns to shape the tale.

Teller develops a repertoire.

Teller has access to an audience.

The community applauds the master teller's skills.[1]

Let's take a look at these criteria for emergence of a master teller as they apply to our ten tellers. When all of these are in place, the teller will often adopt the social identity of storyteller. And once that identity is embraced, the teller's path down a lifetime of continued storytelling is set.

Why Do They Become Tellers?

Hearing Tales as a Child

The tellers speak at length of the stories they heard in their youth. Lela says of her Eskimo father, "He told us *sooo* many stories." Léonard tells us, "I learned stories by listening to my grandfather and my grandmother." Won-Ldy explains that he heard stories every night from his grandmother. Roberto Carlos tells of the importance to him of those tales he heard from Sahita, the orphanage cook. Phra Inta speaks of listening as a child to an old man in his village tell stories.

Assuming the Role of Active Teller

The shift from passive listener to active teller came at various stages for our tellers. Won-Ldy was trained as a child to begin telling. He reports that by the seventh grade he was already performing in public to great acclaim. By the time Rinjing was in his late teens, he was already styling himself as a raconteur, offering his humorous tales to his friends to their great amusement. Roberto Carlos didn't come to telling until he was a young man, when he began to teach and realized the usefulness of this tool. Vi Hilbert began to share stories much later in life, also as a teaching tool. Makia discovered his storytelling talent in his forties while doing cultural work with a parks department program.

Adopting Tales as a Means of Personal Expression and a Validation of One's Own Attitudes

Won-Ldy seems especially clear about this. He considers the storyteller to be the "defender of the peace." The morals for the community are laid out by the teller. "So if *you* are going to be the one who will set the value of things so people will be moral, then you must think yourself about your own actions." Rinjing tells his bawdy shepherds' tales as a way of validating his own persona in a Western culture that expects religiosity of Tibetans. Makia's telling took a remarkable leap forward when one day he dropped his "proper" talk and jumped into his own familiar pidgin. "All of a sudden, out of sheer panic, I switched the whole thing into pidgin!" Now the tale could express the real Makia. It could validate his contemporary Hawaiian self.

Developing Storytelling Skills

Though each teller obviously possesses certain natural storytelling abilities, all have honed their storytelling skills through years of performance—some with small groups, some moving on to mainstage festival performances.

Both Won-Ldy and Roberto Carlos speak of specific storytelling techniques they employ, showing their very conscious choices with technique. "I would walk around [the street] sometimes and watch," says Roberto Carlos. "Just notice the different ways that people who tell stories would tell tales. So I really incorporate the tricks of the people I watch." Those who do main-stage work have all developed strong voices, good projection, and clear enunciation. Some, such as Won-Ldy and Roberto Carlos, use large body movements. Others, such as Vi, Lela, and Phra Inta, stand or sit with still-ness, as is their custom. Curtis plants himself in one spot but through use of his drum or talking stick evokes a good deal of motion.

Connecting with the Audience

All of our tellers clearly give thought to connecting their tales with their audiences. Phra Inta speaks of reviving the old tales in attractive ways to engage his contemporary audiences. Léonard Sam struggles to make the stories as user-friendly in French as they are in his native Kanak, bemoan-ing the fact that children today cannot enjoy the tales in their original lan-guages. Won-Ldy refers repeatedly to his connection with the audience: "Now if you can *handle* your crowd, if you can *play* with it, so the audience sees you have the *fun,* the audience automatically starts to enjoy it. That's the biggest secret about me performing."

Shaping the Tale

Though our tellers give strong nods to the traditional tellers from whom they first heard their tales, they clearly make artistic choices in shaping the material for presentation to a contemporary audience.

Curtis uses the unusual technique, probably that used in his family, of providing several minutes of introduction to each story—more or less talk-ing his way into it. A deep breath signals that he is starting the story. But even within the story he stops at times for chatted asides about elements of the tale—explaining, for example, how animals listen. And his tales end with no fanfare whatsoever, a disconcerting device for his non-Indian audiences, who don't realize for some time that the story has ended. Within the telling he uses the story plot as a structure on which to hang his contemporary improvisations. In each version of "Coyote and the Field Mice" the mice were eating goodies, but Curtis improvises their snacks differently with each telling, perhaps matching his own most recent gobbling of goodies.

Makia has spent hours honing his stories. Some, such as "Katie's Store" and "Guava Man," have been shaped into prose poems and have assumed a finished form from which he no longer deviates. He wants every word to be perfect. And he delivers these pieces with great effect, knowing exactly how to use his tone and his pauses to move the audience. His humorous tales tend to be offered more freely, as he remembers slightly different details with each telling, reliving the event with a fresh joy each time he tells.

The various tapes of Roberto Carlos's tellings show him constantly honing these pieces—working with the parallelism, finding even more exciting ways to engage the audiences. The timing of his trademark "jump" tales is already perfected to a "T."

Phra Inta, Vi, and the others all clearly have shaped their tales through many retellings to arrive at pieces that constantly delight their listeners.

Developing a Repertoire

Adams notes the importance of developing a repertoire broad enough to meet the demands of varying storytelling situations. His subject, Mrs. Watanabe, prized herself on having just the right story for any occasion. Won-Ldy's tradition carries this need to a high standard. The Dan teller must be able to tell just the right story to help solve the community's dilemmas. Won-Ldy's working-folk repertoire is not this broad, however, consisting of a dozen or so children's stories. He expands this repertoire often by tossing in humorous personal stories he has shaped. This troubles his sponsors at times, but he points out that the improvised story is a highly prized art form in Liberia. Vi has constantly expanded her repertoire through transcribing ever more stories from the University of Washington archives. And, as noted, she has at least on one occasion added a story from another culture that she felt matched her audience's needs. Early in his career of school and park performances, Makia introduced into his repertoire several Hawaiian folktales taken from books. Once he pidginized these, they were fun additions to his repertoire. But Makia's own personal stories of survival are important tales that audiences need to hear. So, the strength of his personal story eclipses any attempts to add in other material. A special problem with repertoire faces Rinjing. The bulk of his tale material is so racy that it is not suitable for American audiences. Even many adult audiences are shocked. This leaves him in a dilemma. He is a fine teller with a large repertoire that does not match the social understandings of his current community.

Finding Audiences

The major factor inhibiting these tellers has been their lack of audiences. It was only in midlife or later that many of these tellers were suddenly thrust into the limelight and rediscovered their heritage of tellable tales. Won-Ldy was a renowned teller in Liberia yet performed in the United States mainly as a musician for many years. Léonard has begun to share his tales beyond the family as museums and festivals learn of his skills. In midlife, Vi discovered an audience in her University of Washington college students. Peter, when faced with groups of children at the Museum of African Art, suddenly began to share his stories. Other tellers, such as Curtis and Lela, have always had family around to enjoy their tales. Both share in public only on request. Their real audience is their own family. As Adams notes, the opportunity to practice storytelling in a reinforcing situation is necessary to the creation of a master teller. Only those tellers who have been gradually exposed to increasingly large audiences have moved into the realm of the platform teller and begun to perform at festivals. This is not to say that these are better tellers than the others, just that their audiences have led them in different directions.

The Community Applauds the Master Teller

Our tellers all have found themselves cast in the role of master storyteller, not only by themselves, but by their communities. Won-Ldy was acclaimed at an early age. "By seventh grade I was already telling stories to big crowds. People would say, 'The kid's a good storyteller!'" As a young man he won awards in storytelling contests in the city. And once he began telling in the United States, he discovered a new market for his skills, which were at that time devoted mainly to drumming. Rinjing says that he was always thought of as a great teller, even back in Nepal. Friends would come over and ask him for his funny tales. Vi Hilbert is not only a respected teller among her people but has also taken on the role of "story encourager." She holds "Adopt-a-Story" events and urges tribal peoples to learn a story from an elder and come share it. Thus, she has passed on the telling torch to many. Makia and his storytelling work are known throughout Hawaii, and his visits to schools, libraries, and conferences are highly prized. Roberto Carlos is well known in Belo Horizonte, Rio, São Paulo, and, with the release of his children's DVD, throughout Brazil.

Why Do They Keep on Telling?

The act of seeking out a fine story, committing it to memory, shaping it for performance, and then putting oneself on the line before friends or strangers to speak the new tale is difficult work. For an individual to tackle this task, there must be strong reason. Some of the reasons noticed in our ten tellers are the desire to pass on and keep alive tradition, the desire to honor one's cultural group, the desire to inspire others, the usefulness of story as an educational tool, and telling for the sheer fun of it.

The Desire to Pass On and Keep Alive Tradition

Vi and Lela have devoted the latter parts of their lives to the task of preserving in print the traditions of their people. Both tell as an adjunct of this work, though Vi has added the task of trying to get younger people to tell the old tales. Her regular "Adopt-a-Tale" parties are one way of doing this. She has trained many young tellers who *are* carrying the tales forward. These folks come not only from her own group but also from several adjacent tribal groups. Vi has also trained non-Indian tellers, such as Rebecca Chamberlain, who carry on her tales. Vi has consistently insisted that the tales *must* be told and that they can be told by any teller who will carry them on—Indian or non-Indian. For this she has received criticism within the Native American community.

Curtis tells his tales specifically in order to preserve them within his own family tradition. His children, who have heard the tales over and over, are expected to be able to share these tales when their time comes.

Though Phra Inta doesn't specifically teach others to tell, he does see his use of story as a way to encourage revival of local storytelling traditions. "These old people, after hearing the old stories, will recall the old stories. And that will revive the old folktales. The old people will retell the stories to their children and their grandchildren. These young people will be interested in old folktales."

Léonard Sam too tells in an attempt to revive interest in the traditional culture. He tries also to revive an interest in his language. "When I tell in the museum, I tell in my language. And afterwards I tell in French. And I tell the people, 'It's great if some of you understand now, and everyone else can try to understand.' And then I will tell in French and they can see how much they really understood."

The Desire to Honor One's Cultural Group

I separate this from the "desire to pass on and keep alive tradition" because several of our tellers are very concerned about honoring their cultural heritage and sharing these tales with audiences yet do not seem to be attempting to "pass the stories on" with the intensity of the efforts of Vi and Lela.

Won-Ldy was trained specifically to carry on his family's griot tradition. But his displacement from his home culture removes him from these duties at the moment. His joy in sharing his Dan culture, though, shapes his life.

Rinjing, Peter Pipim, and Makia are concerned that their specific cultures be represented and honored in the eyes of others. "It seems as it I took it on as my . . . my cross . . . my crusade . . . to talk about Kalaupapa," says Makia.

The Desire to Inspire Others

All of our tellers would probably say that they tell stories to inspire others. But for some this seems to be a basic reason for their telling, at least for some elements of their repertoire. Phra Inta's stories, of course, are shaped to carry moral meanings to his Buddhist congregation.

Makia clearly tells in order to create a more humane attitude toward Hansen's disease. He also tells with the express notion of encouraging others by example. He tells of the girl who had no intention of going to college. After his presentation she went back to her advisor. "'If he can do it, I can too.' It's that kind of message the kids pick up," says Makia. "I mean we don't tell them, right? They just pick it up on their own." He continues: "And they read the message . . . the other message . . that it's not the stories I'm telling. It's the fact that I'm standing in front of them."

Roberto Carlos too shares his life story to inspire others, especially young teens. He shares his story with youth groups, in detention facilities, and one-on-one with the teens he sees struggling. As he says, "I discovered the power that words could have over me, and over other people."

Many of Vi Hilbert's tales point a direction to moral behavior. After noticing that she had added a tale to her repertoire from a neighboring culture, I realized that she was selecting tales specifically for their importance—tales children needed to hear.

The Usefulness of Story as an Educational Tool

All of our tellers use story as an educational tool. But some seem particularly conscious of this. The use by Phra Inta and Vi of the moral tale has already been mentioned. Roberto Carlos began using stories specifically to aid in his high school classrooms. Peter Pipim and Léonard Sam adapted tales for use in their museum educational work. And one sees constant educational insertions within the tales Curtis tells. Clearly he is using story as a vehicle to teach many things about tribal life.

Telling for the Sheer Fun of It!

All of these tellers are having a very good time at their telling, or they would not keep doing it. But in particular I was struck by the sheer joy found in this art by Won-Ldy, Rinjing, Roberto Carlos, and Makia. These four seemed nearly bursting with delight every time they launched into a new tale. As Won-Ldy says, "I *play* with the art. When you are looking at me, you forget that I am talking to you. It is like I am dealing with *myself.* I am *there.* I am playing by myself. I am having *fun!*"

All of the reasons discussed probably have a part in each teller's motivation to share tales. These tellers have chosen to devote large amounts of energy and time to this art of storytelling. For their incessant work and eager tellings we must thank them. Our world is a more delightful place today because of the story gifts these tellers share.

Note

1. Robert J. Adams, "Social Identity of a Japanese Storyteller" (PhD diss., Folklore Institute Indiana University, September 1972), 65.

12

How Traditional Are These Tellers?

The term "traditional storyteller" usually refers to tellers whose repertoires were passed down from others and who share their tales within their own communities. When a teller begins to share tales beyond the close community, when a teller begins to add to her or his repertoire from books or other traditions, when a teller becomes a part of today's revivalist storytelling movement, can this teller still be considered "traditional"? Let's examine this question.

The Revivalist Movement

A large and thriving storytelling movement exists today whose tellers seek out tales from many cultures, create their own imaginative stories, shape personal stories, and draw from literary sources for material. We call these tellers "revivalist tellers." This term notes the fact that many of these tellers breathe new life into tales found frozen in print. They "revive" the tales.

The revivalist storytelling movement has grown rapidly in the United States and Canada since the inception of the National Storytelling Festival in Jonesborough, Tennessee, in 1973. The organization that sponsored this festival quickly grew to more than seven thousand members, including not only full-time storytellers but librarians, teachers, ministers, health care providers, and others. Though librarians and teachers have been reviving stories from books to tell for decades, the emergence of NAPPS, the National Association for the Preservation and Perpetuation of Storytelling (now renamed the National Storytelling Network), brought about a growth of freelance tellers. These individuals attempted to make a living by telling stories. Schools began to hire tellers for assembly performances and workshops. Public libraries hired professional tellers to supplement the work of their own librarians. A market for storytelling workshops taught by professionals grew as educators, librarians, health care professionals, park rangers, religious leaders, and even the business world recognized the value of a well-told tale. Bringing all of this to the eye and ear of the public were the many storytelling festivals that sprang up around the country.

Platform Tellers

Tellers taking the mainstage at these festivals needed to develop a new set of skills. In the larger venues tellers speak through microphones, on stages raised high above their audience, sometimes blinded by spotlights that prevent eye contact with their listeners. Thus a new term was created: "platform teller."

There is a desire among the producers of today's storytelling festivals to present ethnic tellers for their audiences. Clearly, taking a traditional teller out of her or his traditional setting and standing the teller up on a stage with a mike and bright lights is not always going to provide a positive experience.

Local producers and storytelling guilds often nurture traditional tellers from their communities. Tellers are brought to perform for small groups, invited to library programs and into school classrooms. Gradually the teller's confidence level increases, and the teller is ready to perform for school assemblies and conferences. Eventually some tellers are ready to take a place on the main stage as featured festival tellers.

Our Tellers

All of the tellers discussed here are now sharing their stories beyond their own culture in schools, libraries, and at conferences. Four of the tellers—Vi Hilbert, Roberto Carlos Ramos, Makia Malo, and Won-Ldy Paye—perform widely as platform tellers.

All of our tellers grew up hearing stories within their own cultures. They still have the works of their elders in their heads. Three of the tellers—Rinjing, Peter, and Won-Ldy—now live far from their cultural homes and strive to share their own cultural memories with American audiences. Four of the tellers still live within the cultural environment from which their stories were drawn: Lela, Curtis, Léonard, and Phra Inta. Two of the tellers now live away from their cultural community but still maintain close ties and visit often. Vi Hilbert lives in the Seattle area but joins frequently in activities on reservations in the area. Makia Malo now lives in Honolulu but maintains a cottage at Kalaupapa and returns there often.

The Traditional Teller as Revivalist

As traditional tellers encounter other storytelling traditions, they discover tales they want to add to their repertoire. One day Roberto Carlos Ramos heard me tell an African tale that I had revived from an anthropological text. A few days later he told this at our festival's ghost story concert! I am sure he meant this as a compliment to me as the author, but I was shocked. I had brought him to the festival to share traditional Brazilian folktales. But then, if a traditional Brazilian teller reshapes and adds to his repertoire an African folktale, does it not now become a part of *his* tradition?

The much-loved Native American platform teller, Johnny Moses, often tells his extended reworking of an Italian American joke. Yet the telling is so imbued with Johnny's cultural persona that one could hardly say it is *not* a Native American tale.

Traditional tellers with eager audiences are often on the lookout for more material to add to their repertoire. In Robert J. Adams's dissertation on Japanese teller Tsune Watanabe, he tell us that Mrs. Watanabe hit a block in her storytelling life when she became deaf at the age of sixty-five and could hear no new stories. She managed to keep adding tales to her repertoire by teaching herself how to read simple kana and borrowing children's books from the school library. She consumed three of these and added the tales to her repertoire. "Even though I can't hear much, and can't tell what people are saying, I can still talk without any trouble. I can talk along a blue streak, *bera bera bera bera,* you know."[1]

Makia tells of trying to learn Hawaiian legends from books. These were mostly rewritten versions penned by haole (Caucasian) authors and lacking the Hawaiian teller's voice. Makia succeeded only when he discovered that he could retell these in his own pidgin and imbue the texts with his own Hawaiian persona. He wrapped the tales in contemporary Hawaiian culture and thus made them accessible once again to both himself and his audiences.

Vi Hilbert tells a beautiful story titled "The Little Basket Weaver," the tale of a girl who has trouble thinking yet achieves through perseverance. It is a useful tale for young people to hear. When I asked Vi's permission to share the story, she sent me a photocopy of the text. It was a tale of the Klickitat people, another Washington state group but not Vi's own. I believe that all of Vi's other stories are taken from her own people. But she was willing to share another group's stories for the sake of a tale that needed to be heard.

The Tradition of Reviving Tales from Text

Some telling traditions, of course, rely on reviving tales from text. The Thai Buddhist monks are expected to retell from Buddhist texts. In northeastern Thailand (Isaan) monks also retell from the lengthy palm leaf manuscripts of local legends that are preserved in the wats. When interviewed, the monks speak of this as their way of learning tales. Yet, in reality, the monks have already spent a lifetime hearing tales told by other monks.

The tradition of retelling tales from printed sources has its roots in antiquity. Nadr Ibn Harith, a cousin of the prophet Mohammed, was a famous storyteller of his time. He brought back to Mecca many Iranian folk narratives that he had discovered while traveling in Iran. It is said that he tried to lure listeners away from Mohammed by telling these Persian tales, which were more exciting than the biblical narratives that Mohammed related. Scholars Mahmoud and Teresa Omidsalar point out that Nadr's stories were in fact learned from books he purchased from Persians, Romans, and others during his travels. The Omidsalars consider Nadr to not be an active bearer of the oral tradition, since his stories were learned from printed sources.[2]

Throughout the ages stories have moved into print and back again to oral rendition with regularity. Theodor H. Gaster, in his book *The Oldest Stories in the World,* tells us that these four thousand-year-old tales preserved in cuneiform were "designed to be heard rather than read. Given the cumbrousness of the cuneiform script, 'books' could not be circulated freely, and reading was something of a specialized art. The tablets were therefore designed only as aids to priests or learned men who recited their contents to the people. Each reciter would, of course, adapt the tale to his particular audience, making additions and omissions at will, and introducing songs at appropriate intervals in order to relive the tedium."[3]

So Who Is Traditional?

We see that defining "traditional" is not so clear-cut. We assume a traditional teller to be one to whom the tales have been passed down orally from others in the culture. Yet traditional tellers often expand their repertoires from many sources.

We assume that a traditional teller is sharing tales passed on within his own culture. Yet tales cannot be confined. If a teller hears a good tale from another culture, his storytelling instinct may well be to add that tale to his repertoire.

We expect a traditional teller to reside within his own cultural home. Yet in today's world, people travel widely and often spend their lives far from their own cultural roots. Are they not still traditional tellers? What happens when a traditional teller no longer has constant contact with his or her own culture? Do we need another term, such as "teller with traditional roots"?

Traditional Teller to Revivalist Teller: A Spectrum

A close glance reveals many gradations of tradition within our tellers. Consider these specific types.

1. *Traditional tellers who live within their mother culture tell in traditional settings within their own culture and have learned their tales from other tellers in the culture.*

Curtis DuPuis lives on the Chehalis Reservation where he grew up. He is willing to share his family stories with non-Indians but feels that his main duty to his storytelling tradition is to share his family culture in intimate family settings. Curtis doesn't tell stories from any other family in his tribe, primarily because he doesn't have permission to do so, but also because learning these tales might contaminate his own family stories. This is the most strict adherence to tradition expressed by any of our tellers, though it reminds us of Vi Hilbert's Aunt Susie, who sat alone repeating her stories daily so as not to forget and get them wrong. Perhaps for her, we need another category: Traditional tellers who have lost their audience.

2. *Traditional tellers who expand their repertoire through tales learned from other cultures.*

Many traditional tellers will eventually be tempted to add tales heard from other cultures to their repertoires. These are heard from a passing traveler or brought back to the community by someone who has traveled. It is thus that folktales have traveled the world so easily.

3. *Traditional tellers who expand their repertoire through tales learned from books.*

As mentioned above, Phra Inta is a traditional teller who relies on printed matter for his tale sources.

4. Traditional tellers who perform within their own culture but in non-traditional settings.

The New Caledonian teller Léonard Sam now tells in school and museum settings rather than in the fireside settings of his youth.

5. Traditional tellers who perform for an alien culture but rely on a traditionally learned repertoire. Lela Oman, Curtis DuPuis, Vi Hilbert, Peter Pipim, and Rinjing Dorje are such tellers. Though Lela, Curtis, and Vi perform at times within their own culture, they also perform for non-Indian audiences. Peter and Rinjing now live in the United States, far from their home cultures. Still, they rely on a repertoire learned back home.

6. Traditional tellers, performing for an alien culture, who expand their repertoires via printed materials, inventions, and tales from other cultures.

We have noted the adaptation of stories from other cultures by Roberto Carlos Ramos and Johnny Moses and mentioned use of printed material as source by Makia Malo. But what of inventions? Won-Ldy Paye often expands his Liberian folktale repertoire by creating humorous personal anecdotes for his audiences. Sometimes his set will consist almost exclusively of a sort of stand-up comedy routine. This seems very untraditional to the American producer of the event. However, in Won-Ldy's storytelling experiences in Liberia, the ability to create stories on the spot was a highly prized skill. So in Won-Ldy's worldview, he *is* doing traditional telling.

7. Revivalist tellers who draw tales from own culture but learn them from printed materials. They share tales within their own culture but in nontraditional settings.

This is the case with many tellers throughout the world today. Lacking the opportunity to grow a strong repertoire from actually hearing tellers in performance, teachers, librarians, and other users of story rely on printed collections of the tales from their culture. Often the teller will have a few stories heard orally from her or his family or from local tellers, but most of the repertoire needs to rely on printed sources.

8. Revivalist tellers drawing mainly on printed materials from their own culture and sharing tales with an alien culture.

Many ethnic tellers living far from their homelands need to rely mainly on printed materials to build repertoires of their culture's tales. Coming from an upbringing within the cultures, these tellers bring a greater sensibility to the material, even though their contact with their culture of origin may be minimal nowadays.

9. Revivalist tellers with some traditionally learned material influenced by traditional sensibilities.

Many, if not most, revivalist tellers incorporate into their repertoire a few pieces that were learned from their own family or home community. For example, I tell a handful of stories learned from my father or other southern Indiana friends. When I share these tales, they are imbued with my own culturally learned southern Indiana sensibilities. At those moments, do I suddenly become a traditional teller?

10. *Revivalist tellers working exclusively with materials learned from printed sources or tellers from other cultures.*

The beginning teller, with a short repertoire of book-learned tales falls into this category. But as this teller's repertoire grows, the teller will most likely soon begin to incorporate stories affected by her or his own cultural backgrounds, and thus become the type of revivalist teller discussed in number 9! And by "cultural backgrounds" we mean not only the teller's ethnicities but also the traditions of the community in which a teller lives, the family in which the teller has grown, and the groups by which the teller is shaped.

After all this analysis, we are further than ever from a definition of "traditional" and "revivalist." Many traditional tellers adapt and revive material from other cultures at times. Many revivalist tellers come home to some material from their own traditions at times.

Perhaps the most important thing to consider when dealing with tradition is that it is always changing. When Johnny Moses adapts an Italian American joke for his repertoire, this is not a betrayal of his culture—it is a playful excursion into an *expansion* of his culture. When Makia Malo turns to a book for a Hawaiian folktale and then reshapes it into a present-day pidgin story, he has not "lost" his culture—he has simply brought it alive for today's audiences. At no time in history has "tradition" ever been pinned to the table like a bug, never to change. The nature of tradition is change. We need to understand that tradition is not "the past." Tradition is the past on the way to the future.

Henry Glassie suggests that "tradition is the creation of the future out of the past. A continuous process situated in the nothingness of the present, linking the vanished with the unknown. Tradition is stopped, parceled, and codified by thinkers who fix upon this aspect or that, in accord with their needs or preoccupations." He speaks of three threads: "one tradition is continuous, running quietly at the edge of thought and beneath common life"; "Another, noisy and conspicuous, is modernization"; "A third tradition is built of recursive work, as people plunder the past to confect new things."[4]

I have titled this book *Ten Traditional Tellers.* And yes, each of these tellers is traditional in many ways. They have learned most of their repertoire from elders and other tellers within their own cultural group. Their performances are shaped by ingrained cultural sensibilities. They see themselves as carrying forward the memories of their elders. And fortunately for us, each has made the effort to open a window for us onto a world we have not previously seen. Thank you all: Vi, Lela, Phra Inta, Peter, Makia, Léonard, Curtis, Roberto Carlos, Rinjing, and Won-Ldy. May you keep telling. And may we keep listening.

Notes

1. Robert J. Adams, "Social Identity of a Japanese Storyteller" (PhD diss., Folklore Institute Indiana University, September 1972), 65.

2. Mahmoud Omidsalar and Teresa Omidsalar, "Narrating Epics in Iran," in *Traditional Storytelling Today: An International Sourcebook,* ed. Margaret Read MacDonald, 328 (Chicago: Fitzroy Dearborn, 1999).

3. Theodor H. Gaster, *The Oldest Stories in the World* (Boston: Beacon Hill, 1952), 9.

4. Henry Glassie, "Tradition," *Journal of American Folklore* 108 (Fall 1995): 395–412.

Index

Margaret Read MacDonald, herself a storyteller, turns a folklorist's eye on traditional tellers in this book and in *Scipio Storytelling: Talk in a Southern Indiana Community* (University Press of America, 1996). She is also the editor of *Traditional Storytelling Today* (Fitzroy Dearborn, 1999). MacDonald, who holds a PhD in folklore from Indiana University, is the author of more than forty-five books on storytelling and folklore topics and has promoted the work of storytellers from Cuba, Thailand, Indonesia, Brazil, and Argentina by soliciting and editing folktale collections of their work. MacDonald was a Fulbright Scholar to Mahasarakham, Thailand, in 1996–97 and continues to travel widely, offering storytelling workshops for educators in Asia, Europe, and Latin America. For more about Mary Read MacDonald, see www.margaretreadmacdonald.com.

The University of Illinois Press
is a founding member of the
Association of American University Presses.

Composed in 10.5/13 Minion
Designed by BookComp, Inc.
Manufactured by Thomson-Shore, Inc.

University of Illinois Press
1325 South Oak Street
Champaign, IL 61820-6903
www.press.uillinois.edu